WHEN TEARS DON'T WORK

Larry Waimon

WHEN TEARS DON'T WORK

Waimon Publishing

First published in the United States by
Waimon Publishing Inc.
7 Quinby Court, Parsippany, NJ 07054
(201) 428-9352

Special thanks to Bruce Nathan,
whose help, planning, and sheer devotion
made this publication possible.

Edited by Stephanie Salomon
Designed by Charles Davey
Printed by Eastern Lithographing Co., Philadelphia, PA
Cover design by Steven Levy
Separation by Digital Prepress Center Inc, Yonkers,
NY

ISBN-0-9618760-1-8

Printed and bound in the United States of America

CONTENTS

ACKNOWLEDGMENTS

When this project was in its infancy, I sought the aid of several corporations throughout the country. All those contacted agreed that this book was indeed a worthwhile project; they were all with me in spirit. Yet when I tried to solicit the funds to underwrite the cost for this venture, suddenly the "spirit" began to disappear. With my deepest appreciation I wish to acknowledge all those participants who *did* give willingly. Without their kindness and generosity, this effort would have been hampered significantly. Their display of benevolence for their fellow man is both encouraging and commendable. My heartfelt thanks to:

The New Jersey Automobile Club
   Matthew J. Derham, President
The American Hoechst Corporation, Somerville, N.J.
   Edward Pinkman, Director of Human Resources, Specialty Products Division. James Houstoun, Safety Manager. Claudette Evelyn, Senior Secretary, Human Resources
The Jaydor Corporation, Millburn, N.J.
   Barry Silverman, President. Stuart M. Balter, Vice President
The Lasky Foundation, Millburn, N.J.
   S. Barnhard, Chairman of the Board. S. Weissman, Vice Chairman. Barbara Wurz, Administrative Assistant. Janice Pravata, Advertising Assistant
Photography by Ernest, West Orange, N.J.
   Ernest and Lorraine Nufrio, Gail, Patty, and Lisa
Graphics Fifty-Five, Clifton, N.J.
   Steven Levy who did the artwork for the front cover.
Pip Printing, Parsippany, N.J.
   Martin Contzius. For all that free copy work of the original manuscript.
Maureen Ogden, New Jersey State Assemblywoman.

ACKNOWLEDGMENTS

Her crusade against drunk driving has not gone unnoticed. The bills she has sponsored are going to save lives—*lots* of lives.

Pat and Donna Ferrante, who founded MADD of Morris County, N.J. Let this book serve as a memorial to Dawn, their daughter, who was killed by a drunk driver, Thanksgiving 1982.

Geraldine Silverman, Drug Awareness Chairman, Millburn PTA. For the constant kick in the pants; it helped keep me going. To her husband Jack for allowing all those family interruptions; you've been a good sport!

The Justin Walder family and the Joyce DeSpirito family. For providing me with the necessary office space. That "alone time" was essential.

Paul Rossey, Superintendent of Schools for the Township of Millburn. Your original critique of my story and heartfelt comments were inspirational and rekindled my resolve.

Joseph Pirrello, Principal of Verona High School, Verona, N.J. For setting up all those lectures. Taking me on that "passage through time" acquainted me with my father's alma mater. Your contribution helped lend authenticity to this story.

Edward J. Higgins, Executive Director of Jersey Shore Addiction Services. For pointing me in the right direction and for opening the right doors.

Father Robert Grady, Associate Professor at Seton Hall University, South Orange, N.J. (AKA Captain Grady, Police Chaplain) and Rabbi Samuel Cohen, Temple Beth Shalom, Livingston, N.J. My thanks to two humanitarians who helped me out of a very bad slump.

Finally, thanks to my good friend and typist, Barbara W. and to U.S. Federal Marshal and friend Arthur Borinsky. As Robert Louis Stevenson wrote: "We are all travelers in the wilderness of this world, and the best that we find in our travels is an honest friend". Thank you both for being such friends.

FOREWORD

He never talked about it, but what almost killed my father during World War II was not the guns of an enemy plane but the eight-word transmission from the control tower: "Come on down, your mother has been killed!" He was an Army Air Corps flight instructor at the time and was in the middle of performing aerobatics for a recruitment newsreel. At the very moment he received the tragic news, the young pilot was entering an inside loop. As a horrified camera crew looked on, the plane fell out of the loop and entered a steep spiraling dive. A mere few hundred feet above ground level, the stunt plane suddenly recovered and my father made a safe landing. As he jumped out of the plane and bolted for the control tower, the camera crew applauded his perilous dive and spin, which they thought was all part of the show. Actually, he never could recall the spin and landing. But he never forgot what he had heard, and later that day he prayed to forget what he was about to see.

Pilot Matt Waimon arrived at the hospital still sporting his helmet and parachute. Shocked, he was led to the emergency room by an ashen, grim-faced policeman, who, like himself, was obviously quite shaken up. Under the blood-soaked sheet lay the remains of his mother, mangled beyond recognition. The convertible she had been driving that day was struck broadside by a young drunk driver who ran a red light. The car rolled three times and his mother was literally ripped apart and thrown onto the roadway. As the panicking driver tried to speed away, he dragged the decapitated body under his car for more than seven blocks, dismembering her limbs along the way.

For many years, I could only imagine what it must have been like for my dad. This was the woman who had brought him through a crippling disability. She was the one who was solely responsible for his later achievements. No son could have loved a mother more. His heart-wrenching grief and the ultimate rage

9

at seeing her killer go free was an experience that had to defy description. Almost as if to acknowledge his frustration and despair, Matt chose to hide the grief and anger and endured both, silently and alone.

I had been on the force for only two years when our family's second run-in with a drunk driver took place. A volunteer emergency unit had just arrived on the scene of an accident. According to witnesses, the unit driver had arrived directly from a party after drinking heavily. He was given explicit instructions not to move his vehicle until I had traffic stopped. The operator disregarded the order and backed up anyway. The big rig struck me from behind, and I was propelled through the air for a considerable distance. The impact gave me severe concussion and caused permanent damage to my spine. The event put me out of work for three months and almost put an end to my police career. The impaired driver resigned as unit driver, though no charges were ever brought against him.

As the years passed, I was lulled into a false sense of security. After all, lightning had already struck our family tree twice; the notion of a third encounter with a drunk driver was too far-fetched to consider. But on the evening of February 9, 1983, all of my preconceived notions were forever shattered. Two fellow officers stood in our family's doorway, a foreboding, unforgettable look on their faces. I knew why they were there. I had stood in too many doorways with exactly the same helpless expression. I knew my father was dead. As the grizzly details became known, our short-lived grief turned to rage—rage at the drunk driver who had struck my dad head-on at over 80 miles an hour and crushed, broken, and ruptured just about every bone and organ in his body.

On that fateful night as I cradled my father's twisted broken body, I finally understood. At that very moment I understood completely just what my dad had been forced to endure a generation before. I understood his years of silent torment and I understood his bitterness and frustration. But most and worst of all, I understood what it's like to be totally powerless to protect the ones you love the most.

This insidious killer, the drunk driver, plays no favorites, displays no prejudice, and shows no mercy, He kills over 70 people a day, claims over 25,000 lives per year, and cripples and maims countless more victims every day, year after year. For fifteen years I had seen the tragic consequences of drunk driving. On that

10

night, I became an expert on the subject and for the rest of my life I'll be haunted and taunted by the memories.

Our sadness and even our anger became overshadowed by a contempt for the very system I had been a part of for so long—contempt for the lawmakers and judge who made it possible for my father's killer to drive drunk even after a prior drunk-driving arrest! Complacency and indifference played as much a part in my father's death as the drunk driver himself. I never tell people that my dad died. I tell them that he was killed—murdered by a man who couldn't control his drinking, killed by a system that wouldn't control the man.

Our family has decided to share with you our personal ordeal and unrelenting torment. I fervently hope that this book will alter your attitude toward drunk driving. But don't expect the "usual" threats and intimidations to make the point. As you will quickly realize, there is nothing usual about this story. Don't even expect the same old point! Drunk driving, getting and staying high, are merely the symptoms. This book addresses the *real* problem: The *Cause!* This time, you are going to be included. If this effort saves just one life, than my father will not have died for absolutely nothing. I sincerely hope that you will benefit from this legacy of our family tragedy. If you fail to heed the warnings, someday you may discover that my book has suddenly become *your* story!

ONE

BEHIND THE MASK

There are a lot of good people out there trying to prevent drunk driving. Yet despite their best efforts and good intentions, people continue to drive under the influence. The latest statistics are discouraging. Drunk driving remains the number one most preventable cause of death in this country. The statistics prove something else as well. Most people really don't give a damn about statistics! To them, all they are is a bunch of faceless numbers. Unfortunately, the blood-curdling documentaries on drunk driving have had little long-lasting impact on the driving public. Intimidating speeches and threats of police reprisals seem to fare no better. I've dramatized this point at every lecture I've given. I tell the group that I have no delusions about what I expect to accomplish and start out by saying: "My words are like a Chinese meal. I'll fill your heads with food for thought, but an hour after I leave, it's 'So what!' and you're empty again!" No one wants to believe that what I say applies to them. After all this time and effort, what is the answer? Why do the warnings go unheeded?

Although it may sound overly simplistic, the reason that people don't listen can be found in just two words: "human nature." We possess an amazing facility to block out life's unpleasantries. Trying to visualize ourselves as either the victim of a drunk driving tragedy or the cause of one are two such unpleasant thoughts. In fact, the notion is so repulsive that we block it out with the oldest trick in the book—denial. We simply deny the possibility of such a catastrophe and write it off as something that only happens to "other people." Nobody wants to admit that they could possibly be "other people." I too denied certain possibilities. I too was guilty of the "other guy" syndrome. But now, after our family's *third* run-in with drunk drivers, I realize that I *am* the "other guy!" Tragically, we just don't pay attention unless the shoe pinches our foot. Until you feel the "pinch," drunk driving will remain a nameless, faceless problem; the "other" person's concern.

In order for my story to work, I must personalize an otherwise impersonal problem. If drunk driving is to be viewed as a real crime, I must produce a real victim, one you can relate to. The victim has to have a name, he's got to have a face, and there must be a sense of loss. And you can't sense that loss unless you first realize what there was to lose.

My dad was a man with an improbable past. He conquered a crippling disability and overcame the prejudices he encountered with a will and tenacity that became his hallmark. His rise to the top of his profession became almost legendary. But too many people came to rely on his expertise. Too many more depended on his generosity and concern. Though he was the victim, too many of us also had been victimized, forced now to go on without him.

This book will acquaint you with the victim. You will peer behind his mask of shyness and humility and discover a man of irrepressible strengths and unending kindness. You will share in the happiness of what once was and realize the sadness of what is no longer.

I've already mentioned that my father had an "improbable" past. Perhaps it would have been more accurate to describe it as being elusive or even secretive. Trying to document his past was like playing that old T.V. game show "Stump the Stars." I kept coming up empty! My mom could only provide marginal assistance and suggested that I quiz my father's sister, Sylvia, his only living blood relative. She filled in the missing blanks and uncovered some of the mystery.

It seems as though their father's dad was somewhat of an 'arty' type—a sort of cross between a Michelangelo and a Paul Gauguin. He was born and raised in Paris, France, and for a living he painted frescoes on the ceilings of wealthy people's estates. Then, like Gauguin, one day he just decided to quit the scene. He packed up his wife and five kids, cruised to America, dumped everybody, and sailed off into the sunset with his new mistress. He was never heard from again.

My grandfather, Charles Waimon, (pronounced "Sharles Vaymón"), along with his remaining family, was left to fend for themselves. His younger brother had cut his leg on the trip over and tragically died from infectious gangrene. The loss, however, strengthened his mother's resolve to provide for her remaining children. Though he was a French Jew, his mother sent Charles to Catholic school. As a single parent, she worked long and hard to afford this luxury, but she was determined to give her son the best education possible. It just so happened that a private Catholic school supplied a better education than its public counterpart. So Charles "Frenchy" Waimon was raised in a convent by nuns—an improbable beginning for a little Jewish kid!

The sisters schooled him well and the young immigrant learned quickly. Not only did he master the academics, but the nuns instilled in him a confidence and self-reliance that would foster his future success. After his schooling, Frenchy began his own business, an automotive supply shop specializing in the sale of "Kelly Springfield" tires. Eventually the business grew to fifteen stores throughout New Jersey. Soon thereafter, he married a very proper lady and they had a daughter, Sylvia; things were looking good. Four years later, my father was born.

It was obvious that something was very wrong with little Matthew. His spine appeared severely deformed and he seemed to be stuck in a fetal position. The doctor's prognosis was pretty bleak. My dad had been born with scoliosis, a malformation of the spine. In those days, orthopedics, if it existed at all, was still in its infancy and there was no real treatment for the disease. For several years, young Matt was totally dependent upon the aid of a very dedicated family and a full-time nurse. Walking, even standing, required constant supervision. A fall would leave him helpless, unable to get up on his own.

All along, my dad's mom refused to believe the dismal predictions of the so-called experts. She simply could not accept the fact that her boy would remain a cripple for the rest of his life. Fed up with seeing her son's twisted little body constantly racked with pain, she decided to handle things herself. She had a forty-pound iron brace constructed for my father's back. It extended from the base of his spine to the top of his neck, to just under the chin. Then she rigged up a harness in his bedroom and suspended him on a meathook like a side of beef! The ritual went on for more than seven years, three times a day, two hours at a time. According to my Aunt Sylvia, the pain was excruciating. Being the good sister she was, she'd maintain a constant vigil over my father during these torture sessions, always trying to cheer him up. She recounted for me this unorthodox form of therapy: "It was sheer hell; the tears would stream from my brother's eyes, but he would never cry out. It broke Mom's heart to watch Matt suffer like he

15

did. All she could do was wait and pray that her son's torment would eventually lead to some improvement."

Seven years later there was not only improvement but outright recovery! The only obvious restriction was limited to my dad's right arm; he couldn't raise it up any higher than his shoulder. Regardless, the results were astonishing and the medical specialists were confounded by the improvement. He continued to endure his iron brace, but mercifully the "hangings" were discontinued.

My aunt continued to unravel secrets of her brother's lonely past. Their family was one of the first Jewish families to move into Verona, New Jersey. To say that he didn't exactly "fit in" at school was putting it mildly. His classmates didn't regard "Jewish" as being the religion of choice, and they emphasized their preferences on my father's face—often! Soon his prominent broken nose was receiving as much notoriety as his bulky brace.

In the worst way, my dad wanted to belong. He wanted to be included, he wanted to be accepted. Yet despite his longings to be like "everybody," he would never take crap from *anybody!* For years, he had hauled around a brace that weighed half as much as he did. That ungainly piece of scrap iron had a unique side benefit. The added weight had served as a portable iron gym. His leg strength had been built up to a level that could only be described as Herculean. When the inevitable fights broke out, he went into battle without the use of his restricted right arm. But his choice of weaponry, though unconventional, proved to be highly effective. At full speed, he'd charge at his enemy like a raging bull. Using his brace as a battering ram, he'd plow headfirst into the unsuspecting adversary. His powerful legs carried the heavy metal with such velocity the impact would knock the opponent off his feet! One unfortunate victim paid the ultimate price for battling this human guided missile. After being knocked on his butt, this upended bully from the football team decided to fight my father in like fashion. He got into the signal set position and charged headfirst into my dad's chest. However, someone failed to inform this poor soul that Matt's brace surrounded his whole upper body, chest and all! Striking the iron armor with his skull, the would-be football star sustained a severe concussion—his season was over!

Eventually, the word got out that Matt Waimon was a force to be reckoned with. Everyone was leaving him alone, with the exception of the football team. But this time, the players didn't want

Charles "Frenchy" Waimon

to hurt him, they simply wanted him to play on the team! He was the perfect running back. Because of the restrictions of his brace, Matt was incapable of any lateral movement when he ran. The only direction he could travel was straight up the middle—and heaven help the blockers that got in his way! When the other teams discovered Verona's "secret weapon," there was a cry of "foul," and my dad's short-lived football career abruptly ended. But this did not deter his athletic endeavors.

The following spring, the brace came off for good. Carrying forty fewer pounds in excess baggage, Matt was now faster than ever. That season he lettered in track. "He ran with a vengeance," my aunt recalled. "It was as though he was getting even for all those years he'd been cheated of mobility." In summer he landed a job as pool lifeguard at Goldman's Hotel, (now Town and Campus, located in West Orange). On weekends he earned extra cash by performing exhibition dives off the three-meter board. One of his greatest fans was the very doctor who had previously deemed my father a "permanent cripple." Every Sunday he would sit at poolside and marvel over young Matt's layouts, flips, and twists. Mystified by my dad's grace and power, the physician could hardly believe his recovery. So as an inspiration to others plagued with disabilities, the doctor requested that the diver perform a very special service. The following Sunday, Goldman's bussed in a large group of kids, all afflicted with polio. Acting like a circus ringmaster, the orthopedist announced each dive over the pool loudspeaker. My father performed flawlessly. About a week later, he received a thank-you letter that was signed by every kid from that ward. Soon after my dad was killed, my mom showed me that letter. "He was too modest to show anybody," she told me, but he was incredibly moved by the simple words on that piece of paper. They said that watching him perform had given them all "renewed hope." They all vowed never to give up trying. They reaffirmed their commitment to work "extra hard" on their physical therapy. But it was the last line of the letter that really touched my father. It said, "When we grow up, we pray we turn out just like you." All his young life, the only thing my father ever wanted was to be just like everyone else. Now, here were fifty-two kids saying all they wanted was to be just like him!

Perhaps it was his new status as community role model, or just his grit and determination. Whatever it was, from that summer on, Dad was determined to surmount any obstacle that stood in

On the road . . . to recovery

his way. Unfortunately, his quest to dive competitively was suddenly thwarted. What made his dives spectacular were his extremely high leaps and close cuts to the diving board. He would delight the onlookers by completing his intricate moves well above the board. But what drew the most gasps were his vertical descents. His signature to every dive was his close brush with the platform on the way down. Old family movies suggest that distances between face and board were often a matter of no more than an inch or two. Then one day, he came two inches too close. He had nailed a beautiful two-and-a-half inward somersault. But he came out of the tuck just a bit too early and plowed nose first into the board. He broke the nose as well as his right cheekbone. Apparently more angry than hurt, my father ascended the ladder once again despite the profuse bleeding. This time he got it right! His poolside doctor friend drove the battered diver to his office, set his nose, and heavily taped his face. The following day, one of the local roughs made light of my father's new looks, likening it to that of a "mummy." The fight was on: the nose was refractured, and his face had to be wired up. The risk of permanent injury now precluded future diving exhibitions.

Undaunted by pain and disappointment, Matt took on his next challenge with a warrior's heart. The track coach had suggested that he apply his quickness to speed skating. Since he had long admired the beauty and grace of the sport, the idea appealed to him. The only problem was that he had never been on a pair of skates in his life. That didn't stop him. Come winter, his self-taught lessons began. Fearing that the kids would laugh at his awkwardness, Dad chose to practice when no one was looking. When his family was sleeping, he'd sneak out of the house and go on down to the frozen pond at Verona Park. On a pair of borrowed speed skates, Dad would practice in total darkness for hours on end, often hiding from the Verona police. Then he would return home, hide the skates in the cellar, and ever-so-quietly slip back into bed.

Skating well just wasn't enough; he wanted to be the fastest and the best. As might be expected, skating all night, and then going to school on just three hours of sleep, was starting to affect his schoolwork. Often he would fall asleep during classes. The teachers usually brought him out of his "coma" with a sharp whack on his back with the yardstick. Night training was becoming increasingly painful! Nonetheless, he kept up the regime. By now the blacked-out skating course was becoming too confining for his ever-increasing speed. He decided to expand his territory. The unchartered area of the pond was riddled with warning signs but they couldn't be seen at night. Fortunately, when Dad took the inevitable "plunge," he was traveling so fast that he skimmed like a flat rock, right back onto solid footing! By the time he made it home, however, his soaked jacket had turned to solid ice. As he shivered in the kitchen, waiting for his frozen jacket's zipper to defrost, a huge chunk of ice fell to the floor. The loud crash summoned his father who charged out with his Louisville Slugger, expecting to bag a prowler. At 4:00 in the morning, there is no such thing as a "sense of humor," and the skates went right into the garbage. The lecture that immediately followed was conducted very loudly in broken French and English.

My father was incorrigible. He regarded his dad's reprisal as just a mild setback. The very next day he located a big old cider barrel about a mile from his house. After several hours, he finally managed to get the barrel up the steep hill that led to home. After disassembling all the barrel staves, he took two of the curved slats and fashioned them into a reasonable pair of skis. Soon, the fledgling skier was schussing down his street. Once again, it became evident that his self-taught method was not always the best way. His "point and go" approach excluded little details such as how to stop! Pease Avenue, where my father's family lived, is perpendicular to one of Verona's fastest and busiest roads, Pleasant Valley Way. By the time Matt reached the bottom of his street, he was going too fast to stop even if he knew how. Dad flew through the busy intersection and struck the opposing curb with the tips of his makeshift skis. His shoes were tied to the wood with lamp wire so the idea of "breakaway bindings" was out of the question. Upon impact, the skis shattered and Dad was propelled into a tree. My father had told me this story himself. He said, "The mishap broke my collarbone. But as I flew through the air, I did flips and twists that I could never do on any diving board!" The driver who avoided striking my father by swerving into a snowbank graciously carried the battered skier home.

More worried about his father's wrath more than his broken bone, young Matt decided to cop a "pity plea." He entered the house screaming as if in dire pain (which he was but wouldn't have shown it). The ploy worked and he avoided his father's anger. Actually, things turned out better than he had hoped.

Contrary to his fears that his father would put an end to his skiing, his father wound up buying him *real* ski equipment—skis, boots, poles, the whole ensemble. I suppose that "Frenchy" finally realized that broken bones or not, proper equipment or not, his son was hell-bent to succeed. For this former cripple, a challenge was nothing more than a game. Dad would tell me, "You meet a challenge but you win a game. But there's no shame in losing, so long as you have tried your best." Regardless of pain and setbacks, he was determined to try his best. Yet as it applied to himself, he seemed totally intolerant of failure. In all his years, there was never a bully, or a challenge that was tougher on him than he was on himself. My father was truly a driven man.

Fortunately for Dad, in his junior and senior year he decided to challenge his mind instead of his body. He studied with the same will and tenacity that he had applied toward sports. By the end of his eleventh year, Matthew had been accepted by New York University, which he attended, majoring in engineering. Eventually, he transferred to Rutgers University in Newark, New Jersey. At Rutgers, he met the woman who was to become his wife. She was Sybil Victoria Sonnenblick, the daughter of an Austrian immigrant. Their first official encounter was a result of a blind date. Ironically, however, they had noticed each other a year earlier at my mother's house. She had hosted a scavenger hunt and one of her friends had invited Matt as her date. Naturally, my parents were amazed by this coincidental second meeting. Mom later confessed that Dad had caught her eye at the party. "He was tall and striking." Your father wasn't a 'pretty boy'; I never cared for those types. But he was ruggedly handsome, broken nose and all, and he wore such fine clothes. Dad loved to wear nice things. He was always well-tailored and extremely well-groomed and I loved his wavy jet-black hair. His classmates used to call him "Dapper Dan" because he always looked like a well-dressed mannequin. Your dad had an air of confidence about him; the same self-assuredness he displayed the night of my party. He studied the clues to the hunt with such intensity and purpose. Then after he read the instructions, he raised his head and managed a faint smile. It was as though the outcome of the contest was never in doubt; he looked like a winner! My only regret was that his date was my best friend."

About a month after their first date, Matt invited his new girlfriend back to his home for dinner. The experience proved to be quite a culture shock to my mother. Mom was an only child who was brought up by parents of modest means. The only way she was able to attend art school (Parson's School of Design in New York City) was on a scholarship that she won at the age of sixteen. Her father was a very hard-working house painter but his income could provide little more than the essentials. Dad's house, by comparison, was considered very stately for its time. The family had a full-time house keeper who served dinner in a French maid's outfit. The table was elegantly set with a handmade lace tablecloth, leaded crystal glasses, fine china, and even starched napkins that were held in place by carved ivory napkin rings. Of course, everyone at the table was properly dressed. During dinner, Mom muttered into her date's ear that he shouldn't have gone through all the trouble. Though she felt flattered, she also felt quite uncomfortable with all the pomp and circumstance. Dad whispered back, "This is the way we eat *every* night!"

After dinner, my father explained how his dad had come to this country with little more than the clothes on his back. He emphasized that whatever they now had was acquired by old-fashioned hard work and talent, and not by the generosity of anybody else. Matt explained that since the Depression his father was steadily losing whatever wealth he had accumulated. Everything he had saved was now being depleted by the demands of some out-of-work relatives, who were subsisting on his dad's generosity. The formality that my mother had witnessed at dinner was a carryover from my grandfather's early days spent in the convent. The nuns and the children supped in very fine fashion. Dress codes and other decorum were closely scrutinized and enforced. The rigidity was just a reflection of Frenchy's upbringing.

I researched the material for this chapter very thoroughly; I wanted to be accurate. There was an old tale floating around regarding my grandfather's legendary table manners. In my quest for authenticity, I was again compelled to call upon good old Aunt Sylvia. She substantiated the bizarre story. In question was a beautiful china teapot, and one sterling silver spoon. My aunt recounted the story. "At every meal, the last thing to be placed on the table was the teapot which was filled with scalding hot water. It was always placed on your grandfather's right side. In it was placed this fancy silver spoon. The rules were simple: If you desired something on the table that was in front of someone else, you would say, 'Please pass me' or 'May I have.' You never, I mean ever, just simply reached for something. If you violated the territorial rights of another diner at the table, you would get the 'spoon!' Quicker than you could say 'Wyatt Earp,' our dad would draw out the silver and apply the spoon to the back of the offender's hand. Slurping soup, chewing with your mouth open, using utensils improperly, were some of the other table taboos." Aunt Sylvia continued, "Dad never really hurt us; it was more startling than painful. Our father engendered *exemplary* table manners and we learned quickly or else! Around our house, *nobody* wanted to be a 'Silver Spoon Baby!' Our father used to say that 'Good manners don't cost anything,' and after all, no one had been poorer than young Frenchy. We had a good upbringing because we had parents who took the time and gave a damn. Despite all the starchiness and blustering, your grandfather was a real sweetheart. A lot of people took advantage of his good nature and kindness. When the economy went sour, people never hesitated to come to him for help. When our father went broke and was dying of cancer, he reluctantly turned to these same people for assistance. But they all turned a deaf ear. He had put them on their feet and they kept on walking the other way; it was a disgrace. Some of those people are still around; how do they live with themselves?"

Throughout the interview, this was the only somber moment. I could see the bitterness in my aunt's eyes when she recounted the story of apathy and indifference. But a moment later, she was jolly and upbeat once again. At least now I knew where my good table manners came from. The legacy of Frenchy's Catholic school upbringing had been handed down to the back of my hand. No silver spoon treatment for me; just a quick rap on the back of the hand with ordinary flatware.

When World War II broke out, Dad elected to quit college; he was determined to serve his country. He tried to get into the Marines but failed the physical because of the limited movement in his right arm. It was the same story for both the Army and Navy. Finally, after demonstrating his physical prowess by performing one-armed pushups for the medical examiner, he was accepted. He entered the Civil Air Patrol, which later merged with the Army Air Corps. In 1980, I tracked down my father's original flight instructor, Royal French Ryder and invited him to be a surprise guest for Dad's sixtieth birthday. This flier, even at eighty-plus years, was as swashbuckling as his name. He had even been inducted into the Aviation Hall of Fame, at Teterboro Airport, New Jersey. Royal gave me his assessment of his former student's ability: "Your father was a natural. He wore a plane like an old coat, always comfortable at the control, always cool under fire. I once watched your dad perform dives for the top brass. He did loops and spins in a plane as gracefully as he flipped and twisted off the board. Maybe that's why Matt was so good at aerobatics. Regardless of the plane's attitude, upside down or right side up, he always seemed to know right where he was. Your father was like a gyroscope; he flew with such great balance. Most of the recruits I took aloft for their first lesson got airsick, but not your dad. I watched his face in the overhead mirror after our first spinning maneuver. Ordinarily, that would do it for most of the green-faced fledglings, but not for him. He loved it and pleaded for more! Matt took to it like a duck to water. If all students had been as easy to train as your father, I'd have been out of a job!"

My Dad earned his wings very quickly. But not all his training had gone so smoothly. In those days, navigation was more of an art than a science. A lot of the flying was done by the "seat of your pants." Today, sophisticated equipment makes I.F.R. (instrument flight rules), a snap. Back then, however, I.F.R. meant "I follow roads!" On his first long-distance solo flight, my father was instructed to follow a landmark. Actually, he was told that if he followed the railroad tracks, he would eventually wind up in the state of Maine. The young pilot followed the instruction and the tracks, with one little exception: he flew south instead of north! By the time he had realized his mistake, the plane was well over North Carolina. By this time, the long-range tanks on the Boeing Steerman had run completely dry. Dad was forced to descend over what he thought was an open cow pasture. The low-lying fog gave the geography an illusion of a smooth surface. But much to his dismay, when the plane broke through the fog, the horrified student saw that he was landing in a grain field that was totally crisscrossed with irrigation pipes. The pipes wiped out his entire landing gear. The base colonel was notified by a very angry, gun-toting farmer. The colonel flew down to appease the man and then airfreighted one dejected pilot back to the base, reading him the riot act the entire way. From this point on, pilot Matt Waimon was nicknamed "Wrong Way Waimon."

Dad pulled a week of KP for that one and was forced to stand guard for as many nights in a persistent freezing rain. Ironically, the punishment was responsible for saving his life. All the extra duty and bad weather had given him a mild case of pneumonia. Dad was taken off flight duty the day he was scheduled for advanced training with an instructor. Another student took his place. The plane was a low-wing two placer. The instructor sat in the open rear hole and the student piloted from the front. The plane took off and rose 100 feet, nosed over, and crashed. Both men were killed on impact. No one fully determined the reason for the tragedy. For a long time, my father felt responsible for the quirk of fate that had led to the young man's death. In fact, the guilt had plagued him so much that as soon as he got his wings, Matt put in for a transfer to a combat outfit. My mom noted, "Though he wouldn't admit it, your father had a death wish. The guilt over that kid was tormenting him. He had died in Dad's place and the only way he felt that restitution could be made was by forfeiting his own life. It took a long time before he got over it." The request for a transfer was turned down. Maybe someone got wise as to his real motivation behind this desire. In any case, his instructor recommended that Matt remain stateside. He felt that his flying talents would be better used in teaching others to fly. The base commander agreed and my father was promoted to instructor.

Soon afterwords the new instructor was granted a leave. When he got home, Matt formally proposed to his girlfriend. But all was not well. His mother informed him that his dad was suffering from terminal cancer. The doctor's prognosis was never made known to his father; Matt's mom just didn't want him to know. Frenchy eventually would suffer through the next seven years before succumbing to his illness. Matt was now grateful to be stationed in the U.S. just in case he was needed by the family.

He was prepared to hear bad news concerning his father. But nothing could have prepared him for the grizzly news that was transmitted by the tower operator. It was August 4, 1943, just ten days before he was to be married. Dad was asked to participate in a short promotional newsreel sponsored by the Army Air Corps. Designed to entice new pilots to enlist, instructor Matt Waimon was told to go aloft and put on a real show. He was dazzling the camera crew with a spectacular air ballet when the words came through his headset: "Come on down, your mother's been killed!"

His high horsepower Waco biplane nosed over and entered a steep spiraling dive. The spins became tighter and much faster as the plane headed for the deck. Everyone watching thought he would crash, but miraculously the spin was stopped, and my father greased in a perfect landing. Of course, the crew on the ground thought that his perilous dive was all part of the show.

The flight he missed . . .
and its tragic result

The base commander who had overheard the terrible transmission from the tower, drove out to greet my father's plane. (Later, the radio operator was punished for his mindless lack of diplomacy and tact.) The colonel drove him to the hospital where his mother had been taken.

In a split second, a young drunk driver had snuffed out the life of his mother, the woman who was solely responsible for Dad's ability to walk. Had it not been for her years of selfless dedication and her determination, my father would have been institutionalized many years ago. He would have been just another forgotten, lonely cripple. His mother had not only given him life, she gave him *a* life, and standing over her grave later, Matt's silent tears acknowledged the difference. Dad's father, however, was not as restrained in his final farewell. This once robust, handsome Frenchman was now gaunt and gravely ill. As the coffin was being lowered, he raised a weakened right arm and shook his fist at the sky. The menacing gesture was punctuated by his repeated one-word question: "Why?" Tormented with unventable anger, he renounced his belief in God, then quietly walked away.

Ten days after his mother's death, Matt married Sybil as scheduled. The occasion was more melancholy than festive. With a war going on, his mother dead, and his father dying, even a short honeymoon was out of the question. The next day the new groom was back in his plane, carving up the skies with a new student. When the lesson was completed, my father grabbed his favorite stunt plane and took off again. The tiny apartment he now shared with his new bride was just off the base. To get Mom's attention, Dad made some low-level passes just a few feet above the building. The roar of the 600 horsepower radial engine did the trick, and Mom ran out scurrying for her life. Once outside, she realized who was doing the buzz jobs and her fear turned to anger. Assured of her undivided attention, Dad pulled back on the stick and stood the plane on its tail. He climbed almost straight up. Mom was able to see that her husband was wearing the gift she had given him the day before, a beautiful white silk scarf that trailed in the breeze, well behind this daredevil. Any remaining anger quickly vanished when my mother realized what he was up to. At 10,000 feet, her pilot husband turned on his skywriting equipment and proceeded to illustrate his love for the young bride. When he was done, Dad had punctuated the heavens with ten wispy little hearts. She was overwhelmed by the gesture but

Pilot Matt Waimon

...and his "lady," Sybil

Pilot-Instructor Matt Waimon fifteen minutes before receiving the tragic news

was more impressed by her husband's resilience. When we discussed this event, Mom declared, "Any other pilot who had gone
through what he had gone through with his mom and dad would
have been grounded for thirty days. But not your father. He just
refused to let anything or anybody beat him. He refused to stay
down. Your dad was a survivor, he always fought back; he was a
remarkable man."

After his discharge, my father set out to make good his wedding vow. He had promised Mom that he would make something
of himself. As far as she was concerned, he already had, several
times over. But Dad was never one to rest on past accomplishments. He had definite ideas of what he wanted out of life and
was specific about what he didn't want. He didn't want medi-
ocrity and he didn't want to take orders; he had had a bellyful of
orders from the military. Three years of taking orders had also
given him a bellyful of ulcers. But the condition cleared up as
soon as he went into business for himself—giving orders instead
of taking them.

His opportunity for being his own boss came when he was
working for a floor-covering company. One of the firm's clients
had recently started a kitchen design service called 'Barmark
Kitchens'. The company founder, Leo Lemchen, was a former
English professor who named the business after his two children, Barbara and Mark. Leo saw in my father the same ability
and desire that had launched 'Barmark'. He immediately offered
my father a managerial position at his Asbury Park, New Jersey,
location. The job only lasted for two years as Leo found him
overqualified for the job of store manager. Matt was offered a full
partnership. With his engineering background and Leo's extraordinary design talents and public relations ability, the two
were a perfect combination. Just how perfect would become evident over the next thirty years.

With Dad's life finally on track, my parents decided to become
parents themselves. Gail was the first, born December 23, 1945; I
followed on May 5, 1948. Charles Edward (AKA "Chucky") was
born several years later, on February 22, 1955.

At the beginning of the chapter, I said that before you can understand a loss, you must know what there is to lose. This meant
an expedition into my father's past. After reading about young
Matt Waimon, you now know just as much as I do about my dad
before he was my dad.That man had been a stranger to me. Of
course, I loved my father, but to love him, I didn't always have to

like him, I didn't even have to respect him. In all candor, I loved him with the same "blind loyalty" that a dog loves its master; completely and without question. In this sense, "liking" is more difficult than the loving. So a more compelling question would be: after reading this episode, can I like this guy; do I respect him?

My father was a young man who had all the reason in the world not to even try. No one, not even the so-called experts would have blamed him if he just gave up. Instead, he elected to endure the pain, the doubters and all the ridicule. He refused to accept mere existence, but chose instead to live, and there is a vast difference between the two. Matt refused any pain killers, he didn't like booze, and he didn't do drugs. He accepted life, he never tried to hide from it.

The next few chapters will serve as a lesson in contrasts. You're going to read about a person who also had to deal with a handicap, though one far less severe than the one you just read about. But this person, instead of embracing life, chose instead to hide from it. This person submitted to ridicule and peer pressure. This man is an impostor, a fraud, a person who existed in a fantasy world while the real one passed him by. This man loses. Take my word for it.

TWO

PRELUDE TO CREDIBILITY

When someone says, "How about some advice?" if you are like most people, you are polite and say, "yes." If you are like most people, you are lying! Most people do not take advice graciously. After all, advice is nothing more than another person's opinion. Accepting that opinion could indicate that your own is either wrong or just not worthy.

Our fragile egos, especially when we are young, cannot accept the fact that we just might be wrong about anything! Being no different, I seldom sought the advice of my elders. When I did so, the results were predictable. As long as the answers were to my liking, I would listen with enthusiasm. But an answer that was contrary to the one I wanted usually signaled the end of the conversation. Case closed!

Somewhere along the way, we all have taken the course of least resistance, the easy way out. So when the bearers of ill tidings threaten to burst our bubble, we respond with the oldest trick in the book; we deny it! Denial is the constant companion of the alcoholic and of the drug abuser who, when faced with the problem, often responds by blurting out: "What problem?" This is the biggest problem—failure to recognize that one exists. Even when confronted by a loved one, this person seldom heeds advice until it is almost too late. At this point, denial may be replaced by acceptance, and thus newfound wisdom. But before we reach this plateau, our lives are impeded by constant bouts of denial. We are willing to hear only when we are willing to listen, and denial, from childhood on, becomes our great protector from "No, you can't," and "No, you shouldn't."

As a kid, if there was one thing I hated more than hearing "advice," it was hearing "No." I fought these two words with the ferocity and stubbornness of the sign I was born under, Taurus, the bull. Just like my zodiac friend, I responded badly when I didn't get my way. All too often I would react by throwing myself to the hard wood floor and then proceed to beat my head into the ground! Not getting my way proved to be a *painful* experience! Eventually, I learned that peaceful negotiation was the better way to argue with Mom and Dad; it also helped hold down the swelling!

Of course, history proved my parents right much of the time. As I entered my teens, I graduated from "No, you can't," and "No, you shouldn't," and advanced right to "See, I told you!" I adopted a more sophisticated form of stubbornness—self-righteousness, a most dangerous element of denial. Wrong as I may have been, false pride would forbid an admission or an apology.

History has a way of repeating itself. In spite of our parent's best efforts, we still make all the predictable mistakes, or more accurately, all the traditional mistakes. Every generation of young people traditionally believes that "theirs" is where it's at. We often regard those who are younger as foolish and naïve, and those who are older (like our parents), as unaware and old-fashioned. It is extremely difficult for an adolescent to relate to an individual who he regards as old-fashioned and out of touch with what's happening. When we cannot relate, we cannot communicate. Once again, history suggests that when communication is removed, what remains is an air of mistrust. Think of how well we relate with the Russians, and then consider all the mistrust. Mistrust among the superpowers, though dangerous, seems unavoidable. Mistrust among our family *is* avoidable, and therefore a shame.

I remember my first day out of the police academy. I was sitting in the squad room waiting for our briefing, when I glanced up at the wall and noticed a poster. It said: "He who does not learn from the past is destined to repeat it." Our parents say the same thing, though not quite so eloquently. They usually come out with, "Only a fool makes the same mistake twice." But in the same breath they often say, "History has a way of repeating itself." To me the statements seem contradictory. On the one hand, the slogan-makers tell us that we should be learning by our mistakes, while on the other, it is inferred that we probably won't. This may suggest that we are either a race of slow learners or we are lousy students of history! On more than one occasion, I have pleaded guilty to both suggestions.

Sooner or later—most likely later—we learn life's essential lessons. But we don't learn them from any history book or from well-meaning friends, or from all the "when I was young" speeches dumped on us by our parents. We learn the way every generation learns, and that is by experience. Experience is still the best teacher. Our folks know this. They too most likely learned the hard way; they too probably refused well-founded advice. As loving parents, they just want to save us some of the heartache and pain that they probably went through. I have come to believe and appreciate the fact that our moms and dads are walking anthologies of knowledge and wisdom. So why, when we were all very young, didn't we tap into their vast arsenal of talent and guidance? Why don't we heed their advice and avoid inevitable pain? Why do we submit to history and always have to learn the hard way? Why don't we listen? This compelling question can be answered in just one word—"credibility." We simply will not listen if what we hear is not credible. As previously mentioned, young people do not often relate or communicate well with their elders which leads to their mistrusting them. It is not possible for mistrust and credibility to co-exist.

Quite innocently, parents teach their children to mistrust them. I for one, credited my existence to the "stork," and looked forward to those nocturnal visits from the "tooth fairy." Eagerly, and without question, I accepted all the childhood myths. But then came that fateful day when one of those famous fables went right into the garbage. The incident occurred in the wee hours of a summer morning. I had lost a tooth the night before and, on my father's instruction, placed the tooth under my pillow. Waking before sunrise, I groped feverishly for the expected bounty. But much to my dismay, what I found was not the quarter (the going rate in those days,) but the original bloody tooth!

In protest, I marched right into my parent's bedroom. An astonished and very tired father reassured me that the "tooth fairy" would come. Encouraged, I trotted off to bed where I maintained a constant vigil on the open bedroom window (screen removed to make her entry easier!). But the only thing to pass through that window were dozens of hungry mosquitoes, and this situation had me scratching (literally) for answers! The quarter finally arrived, but not on the wing, or through the window. It came on a pair of very mortal legs, clad in some very familiar pajamas, answering to a very familiar name—Dad!

From that day on, my father's credibility began to wane. I started to wonder if the tooth fairy idea was a fake, could Santa be far behind. But aren't all our childhoods filled with such little "white lies?" As harmless as they appear to be, they often set a precedent that comes back to haunt even the most loving of parents. A kid gets confused by misleading information, or no information, and this can create a climate of mistrust. How often were you told not to do something by one of your parents. You asked, "Why?" The answer was such as, "I'm your father and I'm telling you so!" or, "I'm your parent and that's all the reason you need!"

Parents are reluctant to admit to their children that they probably made the same foolish mistakes and assumptions that we all make; maybe they are too ashamed, maybe they are too embarrassed. Whatever the reason, their intentions are usually noble. They simply wish to protect us from similar hurts. In the name of "protection" they often feel justified to respond with overly simplistic answers and remedies. They want replies and orders to be accepted and carried out on mere say-so. Up until a few years ago, I, (if I had a child) would have expected or demanded the same—blind loyalty or blind obedience. Do it all without a question. But in reality, this sort of expectation just doesn't work. I remember an appropriate saying about dealing with difficult problems. It went like this: "Beware of simple solutions, they reveal a simple mind!" Most parents are not simple-minded, even though at times their answers leave us flat. If only they were more upfront about their own past mistakes and shortcomings. Perhaps then, we would have been more inclined to listen and less inclined to make the same mistakes.

When I started lecturing on "drunk driving" I made some significant mistakes in my approach. Because of vanity or embarrassment, I told the students almost nothing about myself or my past. Since I was an authority figure, I wanted and expected my points of view to prevail over theirs, merely on a familiar "because I say so" basis. I had made a tactical error. Like the parents that I had described, I was providing simplistic solutions to a very real and tragic problem and was receiving for my effort the kind of response that I deserved: blank faces and utter indifference, and why not? I had not been addressing the real issue. It is not drunk driving. Drunk driving is just the symptom of the more serious problem, the cause, or what makes us drink in the first place. What compels us to do drugs, to seek escape, to constantly look for that which does not exist? The search starts when we are young, very young. So do our problems, which can persist and exist throughout our entire lives.

Ever since I was very young, I have been an escapist, a seeker of that which does not exist. I have been the perfect candidate to become an alcoholic, a drug abuser, a society drop-out. Even to this day, I wear the sign of a "dreamer" around my neck, a gold carving of a Japanese character known as "Yume." I was honest enough to admit what I was, I just would not admit it in English! In other words, I wasn't willing to admit it at all. But I realized that if I were going to make a difference, if I was serious about making this difference, I had to opt for full disclosure, no more half truths. I had to address the cause, and at any cost, ego not-withstanding, I had to qualify myself as an authority on that cause. In short, I had to cut the crap!

The next time I spoke at a school, I was prepared. More accu-rately, I was prepared to tell the truth, to withhold nothing. This time, I did not speak from the perspective of the knowledge gained from past mistakes. Instead, I told the students what those mistakes were, and how they hurt me and what they taught me. I spoke about my childhood need to be accepted, to be included. Then *we* not *I*, spoke about "peer pressure," and "fear pressure;" the major cause for taking that first drink, that first toke, that first "toot." Suddenly, we were communicating. Suddenly the looks on their faces were not the looks of vague indifference, but of in-volvement and concern. Suddenly, everybody was listening!

There was a vast difference between this lecture and the one that preceded it. I had gone to that school, like the one before, with my guard up and my uniform on. My appearance and my age is what intimidated them. The way they spoke and their youth is what intimidated me. We were suspect of one another. But as soon as I stopped searching for a way and simply started telling the truth, we all discovered a dialogue that transcended the gen-eration gap. I had gone to that school to *teach* something; I left that class having *learned* something. From that time on, I would never underestimate my audience or their ability to recognize and respond to the truth.

Since my crusade began, I have spoken to thousands of people at schools and corporations throughout the state. I still tell it like it is, and often the audience's reaction is just as candid. But one of the most typical responses is still the one that leaves me a little perplexed. It is when the listener approaches me at the end of the presentation and says: "Gee, under that uniform you're a *real* person!" My response to them? "Gee, I thought I *always* was!"

But I know what they really mean. People have a preconceived notion of what a cop is supposed to be—the stereotype of the old

PRELUDE TO CREDIBILITY

Hollywood cop, tough, insensitive. But instead, I throw them a real curve and introduce them to "Larry," not to "Officer Waimon." They quickly see the "person," and what I'm wearing seems inconsequential. They *believe* me.

If you were to tell me something you expected me to believe, I would have to know more about you. If you're going to believe in what I'm trying to tell you, you're going to have to know more about me. The next chapter has nothing to do with drunk driving, specifically, yet it is the most important chapter in the book. For you to listen to my "advice," for you to relate to it or see something of yourself in it, my story must be "credible."

THREE

CROOKED MOUTH

Some of the more lighthearted anecdotes in this chapter resulted from my close friendship with the Bertsch family. Mrs. Bertsch died suddenly on December 5, 1982. She was a loving wife and a mother who was there for her children. Dorothea Bertsch was also a physical therapist who constantly attended to the needs and sufferings of others. She was a modest lady, a very giving lady, and she is sorely missed.

In the last chapter, I described my legendary childhood temper tantrums, those bouts of "head smashing"—the skull to hardwood floor variety. But the first time my head hit the deck, it was totally unintentional. Mom was in one room doing laundry. I was eighteen months old, in another room, doing I-don't-know-what. Suddenly, she heard a blood-curdling scream and dashed into my room. There I was, flat on my back, lying in a huge pool of blood, having fallen backward onto a toy metal truck. As loud as she could, Mom yelled for her downstairs neighbor who happened to have been a registered nurse. She also had a car, (my mother didn't drive at the time). The two worked on the wound but quickly realized that they could not stop the bleeding. They threw me into the car and proceeded to the nearest hospital. The doctor in Emergency informed my mother that I had almost died from the loss of blood. All the bleeding was from a tiny little gash behind the left ear but it had broken a major blood vessel. A few stitches later, a transfusion, and soon I was back home. That night, when she went to look in on me, she noticed that I was sleeping but with my left eye completely open, never blinking, never moving. The next day, we went back to the doctor, but this time to our trusted family physician. The prognosis came quickly and it was pretty bleak. Though the wound was small, it had permanently damaged the nerves that controlled the left side of my face. The doctor told my mother that the entire left side of my face was completely paralyzed. He went on to say that because I could no longer smile, blink, or frown, the left side would be forever devoid of any emotion, lifeless.

But like my father's mother, both my mom and my dad refused to accept the doctor's grim forecast. Plagued with unfortunate and unrelenting guilt, my parents dragged me from one specialist to another, week after week, month after month. The doctors did everything but help me. But my parents, regardless of the financial burden, were determined to find a cure. On the advice of one doctor, I started an experimental form of therapy. Every other day for three years, a Red Cross station wagon would pick my mom and me up at the apartment and drive us to the hospital. Once there, I would be placed on the treatment table and a huge infrared light would be switched on. It was directed at my face and I would remain on the table for approximately an hour. But this was just the warm-up. After my face was sufficiently baked, the nurse would go to work on me with what can only be described as a miniature electric cattle prod. The hand-held unit produced a buzzing sound along with its mild electric shock. For the next half hour my left cheek would be prodded and stimulated in an effort to get the facial muscles to work again. But for several hundred treatments, all it ever did was to make my face twitch and my left eye blink like crazy. After the third year of being warmed, baked, and electrified, the treatments were discontinued. The results? No change, no improvement. No longer concerned about remaining in the neighborhood of the hospital, we were free to move to our new home that had just been completed on Hazelwood Avenue, in Livingston, New Jersey. It was much closer to Dad's business and was considered a great area and a nice suburb in which to raise a family. It was expensive for us at the time though—$16,000.

Until I started school, my condition never bothered me. I only had one friend at the time and he didn't seem to notice or care. What's more important, I did not seem to care. It was not as though something had been taken away; I was just too young at the time to have remembered what a straight smile or an eye that blinked ever was. You don't miss what you never really had, and Mom and Dad were very careful not to point out the differences. There was no pity, no preferential treatment; I had felt normal because I was treated normally. But with the first day of kindergarten, I discovered just what "normal" was, or more accurately, what it wasn't; it *wasn't* me!

That first day of school proved to be more traumatic than the accident itself. Within the first few minutes of class, I think everyone had asked me the same questions: "What's wrong with your mouth?" "What's wrong with your eye?" "Why is your mouth crooked?" I couldn't get out of that school fast enough. I decided to casually slip out the door, but my escape was thwarted by the principal. I told him that I was lost. By the hand, he escorted me back to a surprised teacher. This time, she was taking no chances and she invited me to be her guest and sit next to her. Suddenly, I was facing the class, and worse yet, they were facing me! This time there was no place to hide and the feeling was unbearable. I quickly excused myself to safer ground, which happened to have been the class bathroom. Once there, I locked the door and refused to come out. I refused to negotiate with the teacher and after the third kid peed in his pants, the teacher rounded up the janitor who helped retrieve me with his passkey. After class, there were some heavy-duty discussions with my parents, myself, and a very bewildered kindergarten teacher. Despite my protests, my parents insisted that I *had* to return to class no matter what. Of course, I responded in the usual fashion, but I soon realized that my head-pounding demonstrations were becoming a futile ploy. Eventually, the inquiries about my face subsided, though not the ridicule that would persist for years to come. But two weeks after school started, the unexpected happened; one of my classmates came up to talk to me, no questions asked. His name was David Bertsch, a cute kid with light, almost white hair, which certainly set him apart from the rest of the class. Perhaps, like me, he felt like an oddity who held himself in pretty low esteem. Maybe he felt intimidated by our classmates and just sought the comfort of someone who posed no threat, a fellow "geek." For whatever reason, I was thrilled to have acquired a friend; it almost made school tolerable.

In a matter of days, David had become my best friend, my only friend. It was ironic that this best friend would be the one to anoint me with a most unsavory nickname. The incident occurred upon my second visit to David's house. After we entered, his mother, upstairs at the time, yelled down, "David, who is it?" He replied, "Larry." Having only met me once, she made the second inquiry, "Larry who?" At the top of his lungs, David shouted up, "Larry! You know, the boy with the crooked mouth!" That explanation made her come running. Obviously mortified by David's accurate description, Mrs. Bertsch made her son apologize for the blunder. I just stood there with that "crawl-under-a-rock" feeling. But in a roundabout way, David's lack of diplomacy and tact turned out to serve our friendship well. He never held back about what he was feeling; he was like an open book, always easy to read. There was no pretense about him so he became not only an honest friend but a reliable one. Nevertheless, his well-founded description of me caught on fast at school. Whenever I heard "Hey, Crooked Mouth," I didn't have to look around to see who they were talking to.

I quickly realized an advantage to our friendship. Once a week, at lunch time, Dave would ask his mom if I could stay and eat. She always said yes, but being the gracious guest that I was, I always stood out in the street until I got the anticipated "wave-in." Mrs. Bertsch was of Swedish descent and she made the most outrageous Swedish pancakes. She made them paper thin, then with a pat of butter on it, she would roll them up into tubes and cut them into neat little sections. Add the syrup and it was pure heaven, or at the very least, a good reason to sustain the friendship. After school, we returned to David's house to catch the "Mickey Mouse Show." But this time, the snacks that were offered were less than spectacular. So as not to ruin our appetite for dinner, Mrs. Bertsch would give us a raw green bean to chomp on. It was hardly what I considered a culinary delight. Never being one to offend my host, I merely pretended to consume the tidbit. The Bertsch family had a black-and-white dog named Terry. As long as the green beans were being doled out, Terry proved to be a real gift. After Mrs. Bertsch left the immediate area, I would casually slip Terry the bean. It was an arrangement that worked out quite well for both of us.

Dave and I had more in common than just our low regard for green beans. We both had, for our own reason, pretty low opinions of ourselves. So together, we created and lived in our own little fantasy world. Every chance we got, we were acting out the latest Walt Disney movie, pretending to be one of the renowned super heroes. One day I would be Kirk Douglas in *20,000 Leagues Under the Sea*. There I'd be, standing there with a makeshift harpoon, poking away at the giant squid. The next day, David would be Captain Ahab in *Moby Dick*. Only David's props were far more elaborate than mine. His grandfather, Mr. Peterson, was a retired carpenter. For David's Academy Award Performance, his grandfather constructed an authentic wooden leg, complete with a carpeted pad on top to rest his knee on. We then turned on a table light that shadowed Dave's figure against the white wall. Our special effects, however primitive, worked as effectively as our imaginations. There, on the wall, was peg-legged "Ahab" harpooning the white whale.

Then came another classic, *Davy Crockett*, another of Disney's doings. Only this time I was determined not to be outdone by my friend's "prop man." This time my parents picked up on some not-so-subtle hints and bought me an authentic Davy Crockett outfit, complete with a genuine coonskin cap. Of course, it was made with genuine plastic and it smelled like genuine ranch skunk! But I didn't care, because now, not only did I look the part of a hero, I was beginning to feel like one. I was even given a genuine cap-firing flintlock pistol to help back me up.

After a while, any hero, real or imaginary, became fair game for our little fantasy excursions. Styling ourselves after our alter egos (what psychiatrists call "projection") was our way of escaping our inadequacies. Projecting myself into the life-styles of those I admired the most turned out to be my salvation from some of the ridicule I had to contend with. In school, I was barraged with constant reminders of my imperfections. But at home, in front of the tube, I became Superman, Peter Pan, the Lone Ranger. I became stronger and bigger than life, more than able to ward off my oppressors, my classmates. Saturday T.V. was what I lived for. When the Lone Ranger yelled "Hi-ho Silver" and rode off to the tune of the William Tell Overture, Mom would haul me away from the box, kicking and screaming of course—an undignified way to have treated a superhero!

Back on the outside, I suddenly felt exposed again, vulnerable. So without delay, I took up my position in the backyard playhouse, built by father. This was my fortress, the place where I stood sentinel over my private little world, my kingdom. I felt secure only within the confines of our property line and was careful not to venture beyond its boundaries. But I was even more careful not to let anybody enter the ground. I was as territorial as the fiercest of guard dogs and almost as vicious! All afternoon, I would lie in wait, anticipating my next intended victim, usually some kid just cutting through. A breach in security however was all the excuse I needed. I would come flying out of my little house and, like some crazed animal, would run up and bite them on the arm or on any other opportune part of the body. But my reign of terror ended abruptly when our neighbor's daughter, wandered onto the grounds while the "attack boy" was on duty. Showing no preferential treatment toward the ladies, I administered a bite to her upper arm that broke the skin. A few days later, the swelling got nasty-looking and finally burst open. Fortunately, the arm healed and there was no one sued. But our neighbor did suggest to my father that I be "leashed and muzzled!"

The next day, in no uncertain terms, my dad informed me that my "yard protection services" were no longer desired. He told me to keep an eye on the *inside* of the house, which I did, literally, every night. But acting as the family "private eye" was starting to play havoc with my vision. Because I could not blink, I could not irrigate the troubled eye. Doctors did not know enough at that time to suggest drops or patching it at night to prevent inevitable damage. The drying had caused a significant astigmatism; I was becoming legally blind in my left eye. In the tradition of treating the symptom instead of the cause, my eye doctor prescribed glasses. But I did not need 20/20 vision to see what my glasses were destined for, and that was *not* for my eyes. One day of wearing them to class, and the fate of those glasses was quickly determined. I was just getting used to "Crooked Mouth" and "Dirty Jew" but "Four Eyes" was just too much! That afternoon, I threw the glasses in a drawer and walked around with an empty case just to pacify my parents. Without realizing it, I had succumbed to yet another form of "peer pressure." Tragically, I allowed others to dictate not only how I looked, but how well I was to see. I didn't mind walking into walls, so long as I looked good doing it. Vanity was quickly becoming a significant part of my life.

By second grade, the battles were growing more intense. I was at a different school with different classmates, facing a different crisis: upper classmen. The only thing that was not different were the taunts and questions that were directed my way. I got to the point at which it was no longer a question of, "Was I going to fight today?", but "*Who* was I going to fight today?" Once again, it was time to quit the scene—runaway time. I ran away so often my teacher had to appoint a special "posse" just to round me up whenever I disappeared. On one occasion, an anxiety attack became so bad, that I ran home and locked all the doors and windows. I would not even let my sister or mother back in. Gail and Mom returned to school and got my sister's teacher to phone my house. After a short deliberation, I did as ordered and opened, as she put it, the "god-damned door!"

Once again, my father was careful not to give me too much sympathy. Many years later, he did confide in me and expressed what *really* had gone through his mind at that time. He said that seeing me constantly frightened and beat up was like watching a rerun of his *own* childhood, a tough-to-watch encore performance that broke his heart. It frustrated my parents to see the effect of the persistent hazings and remain unable to intervene. Nevertheless, my father had the strength to match his wisdom and allowed me to "grow up," lumps and all.

Once, however, I did catch him cheating. On my way to class, I noticed the school bully lurking behind his favorite tree. As I passed by, pretending not to notice him and praying that he hadn't noticed me, something very strange happened; nothing happened! No ambush! Breathing more easily, I couldn't resist a wondering look back over my shoulder. All I could see however, was the back of this bully pressed firmly against the trunk of the tree, his feet dangling a good yard off the ground. Helping to create this illusion of the "Levitating Bully Trick" was the very strong arm of one very angry father! Apparently, my dad had been riding shotgun over my morning treks to school. For some time, he had watched me run the gauntlet, always careful to avoid detection. Understanding my need to feel self-reliant, he would never intentionally rob me of my dignity. But this time, he kept me from being robbed of my teeth—a fair exchange for just a little "dignity." After the brief chat with "Hulk Jr.," the kid came running by me as if I wasn't there. He looked scared. My father's form of curbside justice had paid off and henceforth, bullies from the "big guy" division kept well away.

Before I was eight, I had developed a full-blown phobia well before phobias were ever in vogue. I don't even think they had a name for it then, but "agoraphobia" is what they call it now. Simply put, it is the fear of leaving one's home. Everything beyond my property line represented a threat to me. My home was my sanctuary, my protection from all outside aggression. So I constantly had to find ways to keep myself entertained, both in and around the house. Of course, there was T.V., toys, and Susie, my sister's doll. But I soon discovered something even more enchanting than all three—matches! I loved playing with matches and quickly became the resident pyromaniac. On several occasions, Mom caught me indulging myself in this new-found hobby.

After the "wait until your father gets home" routine, the threats became more elaborate. She tried to make good on one such threat. Catching me with yet another lit match, she promptly lit up one of her own and, as promised, was about to administer justice to the offending fingers, after she blew out her match of course. (She only wanted to scare me, not scar me!). She succeeded, and I bolted for the door, Mom in "hot" pursuit, still clinging to a much cooled-down match. But I wasn't taking chances. After the second lap around the house, Mom was gaining ground. So as soon as I turned the corner, I immediately lay down on the slate walk. Realizing that drastic times call for drastic measures, I pretended to have fallen in hopes that I could cop a "pity plea" in order to avoid punishment. The ploy worked, but not my mother's deterrent. My final escapade took place just a week later. I was in the den playing with my little brother Chuck, just about one year old at the time. The baby sitter, "Mrs. Big" (a 250-pounder who earned the nickname), was in another room. With the coast clear, I put Chucky down and picked up my hidden stash of matches. One lit match got away from me, fell and promptly ignited the linoleum. I was able to stomp it out and clean up the mess. A shocked Mrs. Big threatened to tell my parents. I had to work fast. After some intense negotiations, I managed to buy her silence with two scoops of chocolate ice-cream. I remember staring at my little brother and crying, thinking on what could have happened. That's what did it; I was cured.

My parents continued to look for distractions for me, but for those of the less lethal variety. One Saturday morning, while making my usual pilgrimage to the T.V., I was intercepted by my dad who presented me with a strange-looking box. I was literally jumping for joy. It was a microscope; something I had wished for but never expected.

The first slide I viewed was that of a tiny red ant—tiny, until I peered through the eyepiece. Suddenly, the ant had become a monster with huge sharp teeth! It was as good if not better than the best science fiction picture I had ever seen at the time. It was also frightening! So, after only a minute of viewing, I elected to study the less formidable fruit fly slide. I was enchanted. I had also discovered a whole new world in which to lose myself to escape. I exchanged hours of looking at the tube for even more hours of looking down a tube. My dad had gotten me away from the T.V., but he had not gotten me out of the house.

The following week, his strategy changed. Counting on my love for entomology, Dad had bought me a butterfly-collecting kit, complete with net and mounting accessories. Since I could hardly catch a winged trophy from inside the house, out the door I went. Now, regardless of my contradictory life-style, I, in the worst way, wanted to be accepted by my peers. That meant that I had to look like them, had to behave like them. But dressed like a refugee from a banana republic, flailing my net at unsuspecting insects, was doing little in the way of winning over new friends. I soon realized that butterfly collecting was not exactly the sport of champions. I quickly doffed the pith helmet and khakis and immediately donned yet another new outfit—a police costume.

Now this was more like it! Here, I thought, was a uniform I could be proud of. After all, the Livingston Police were right up there with Superman and the Lone Ranger! So, with badge securely in place, I went off on patrol. Alas, my tour of duty was extremely short-lived. Feeling all-powerful, I wandered three blocks away from my house, which for me, was definitely out of my precinct. Standing on a corner were two boys whom I had never laid eyes on. They were both much bigger than I was, but that did not matter; I was a cop, a force to be reckoned with! Approaching them from behind, I shouted out my first official order, "Hey, turn around"—which they did immediately. It felt great, they actually responded to my command. But then I got badge-heavy and made a big mistake; I gave them a second order! I said what cops were supposed to say in those days; I told them to "Move!" I didn't know where to; I didn't even know why; I just said it. Unfortunately, the two strangers had no intention of participating in my fantasy. Suddenly, I felt that I had chosen the wrong career. But instead of receiving a punch to the face for my indiscretion, they did something much more painful; they laughed at me and then took my hat. All I could do was to turn tail and run.

Once back on home turf, I made a beeline right for the security of the old playhouse. But suddenly, I heard an ear-shattering scream. Looking out the window, I saw my childhood girlfriend, Joanie Traphagen gesticulating wildly. I immediately thought it was my chance to redeem myself as a police officer. I flew out the door and headed right for this damsel in distress. But when I saw what was making her scream, I kept on running—in the opposite direction! She had inadvertently stepped right into a nest of angry yellow jackets and was covered from head to toe! Frantically, she started chasing me around the house, pleading for me to help.

Not anxious to be a part of the stinging frenzy, I just ran faster! Fortunately for Joanie, good old Mom, who heard the commotion, came barreling out the front door. She grabbed the terrified girl by the arm and immediately peeled off the infested clothing. Mom had thwarted the attack, though she too was stung repeatedly. But she didn't even flinch or cry out. It was the bravest, most selfless act I had ever seen. I was very impressed; very proud of this quiet lady who had displayed so much courage. As for me, my self-esteem had dropped to a new low. I had disgraced the uniform, not to mention myself. Disgustedly, I tore off my police garb and tossed it in the garbage. Thirteen years later, I would be reminded that a mere uniform does not make a policeman.

Eventually, I did find an outfit I was comfortable with. I became a Cub Scout and there was something very wonderful about wearing a uniform that so many other kids were wearing. What it was could be found in the definition of the word itself. "Uniform"—alike, similar. I loved the uniform because it made me look and feel just like everyone else. I suppose it was like being an ostrich in reverse. The big bird sticks his head in the ground, hoping that no one will notice his body. I camouflaged my body in hopes that no one would notice my face. It seemed to work out well and most important, for the first time, I felt included. There was yet another benefit to being a Cub and that was that I got to see my father more often. He was building up his business at the time, often working sixty to seventy hours a week. His rigorous work schedule left precious little time to be together. But every time there was a pack meeting or a father-and-son dinner, he would drop everything to attend. I knew that these times would be short-lived, but it was at the very least, "quality" time. It did not seem to matter how tired he was or that the food at those dinners was not that great. He would just sit there, smiling away with his arm around my shoulder, singing those trite little scout songs, always just a little off-key. Whatever was lacking in my life at the time, I certainly never lacked for a pair of loving parents, who simply, gave a damn.

With the beginning of third grade, school actually started to intrigue me, and so did the teacher—well, actually, *just* the teacher! Ann Sullivan was beautiful, twenty-two years old, on her first teaching assignment, and my first love. No doubt about it, I was smitten! No more running away from school for me. Now the school had a different problem; how to get me to go home. I looked for any reason, any excuse to stay after class, just to be around her. In the morning I would wait by her empty parking space, anxiously anticipating her arrival in that old station wagon. I was her self-appointed valet, ready to carry her books along with my very large torch. My friend David also had a mild crush on Miss Sullivan. Together we devised an elaborate scheme that was sure to win her over. We knew that our teacher drove home the same route every day, right past David's house. As soon as her jalopy rounded the corner, we would immediately stage a mock fight. We were like two knights, jousting for the affections of our fair maiden. Miss Sullivan was less than impressed—so much for chivalry.

But I would not be thwarted. Since I couldn't fight for her attention, I figured that I might try dancing for it. There was a class play coming up. Miss Sullivan was looking for male dancers to do a calypso dance number. Dave and I were the first to come forward. We immediately got the lead parts and with it, the added bonus of after-school rehearsals with my older flame. Then came the night of the big performance. Everyone that mattered was in the auditorium waiting for the show to begin. Suddenly, disaster struck! David had developed a profuse nosebleed. He got them often, and this one was most likely brought about by an anxiety attack. If only he could have shown fear like the rest of us and just peed in his pants! The performance was about to begin, but there was no way that David would be able to go on. This meant that there was no way I was going to go on without him. By this time the calamity was holding up the performance. Miss Sullivan was giving me the old "the show must go on" speech. But with tears in my eyes, I delivered my final words: "No Dave, no dance." Cool under fire, Miss Sullivan dispatched another teacher to summon Mrs. Bertsch from the audience. She soon arrived and was able to ebb the tide of blood from her son's nose. After some plea bargaining, David reluctantly agreed to perform. The show *did* go on. We were not the best dancers Monmouth Court School ever had, but with David's blood-soaked costume on center stage, we were the most colorful!

The following year we moved into our new home, on Dawson Terrace, in the same town. It was a much larger house, equipped with a two-car garage and three bathrooms. These amenities in 1958 were considered luxuries. The bathroom Gail and I shared even had a double sink, which put a halt to the early-morning battles. The kitchen was designed by Dad and was nothing short of state-of-the-art. Eventually, it even appeared in an issue of

"Defender of the wild suburbs" with my sister, Gail

As my childhood hero, Davy Crockett

My seventh birthday party. From *left to right:* (unknown, unknown), Larry Waimon, (unknown), girlfriend Joanie Traphagen, David Bertsch

The father who was there for us

No more bullies.

Building up . . . to fight back

House Beautiful. Things were definitely looking better for us. My father and his partner had expanded their business and Barmark Kitchens had grown to include three more locations. The business had become one of the biggest design services in the Northeast. It appeared that all my father's labor was finally paying off. Everyone seemed happy except me. I had moved less than one mile away from my best friend, but it might as well have been one hundred miles. We were now attending different schools and we got to see each other very infrequently. Once again, I was friendless; once again I was on the outside, peering into a world I didn't quite fit into. It was back to being alone, back to the life-style of self-imposed seclusion.

With the business doing well, dad decided it was possible to finally take some time off. For the past twelve years, with the exception of a few long weekends here and there, he had never taken a real vacation. The few times we did get away, it was to go to some fancy hotel where I bellyached about having to put on a suit for every meal. It was a real drag for a kid my age; all I saw were old people with shuffleboard sticks in their hands or blankets on their laps.

But thanks to my parent's close friends, Dick and Eleanor Barrett, the vacation scene was about to improve dramatically. Upon their suggestion, we agreed to vacation together at their favorite spot—Lake George in the New York State Adirondacks. As we drove along the lake, I caught a glimpse of something strangely familiar. Perched high atop the road sign for the Still Bay Hotel, overlooking the bay and ready to spring from its wooden stand, was a painted carving of my old childhood hero, Peter Pan! We had not even arrived at our destination and already Lake George was looking pretty good. It was like some kind of omen, a forecast of things to come.

A few moments later, we arrived at what was to be our home for the following week. We drove through the big iron gates of the resort, the Gate House and were greeted by the proprietors who promptly showed us to our two-bedroom cabin. The rustic, immaculately kept cottage was a far cry from those stuffy, uppercrust hotels of years past; it was great. An hour later, Neal (the Barrett's son), and I were on our way down to the lake, armed to the teeth with fishing gear. In all the years past, I had never been able to catch a single fish, so I was not too optimistic. But much to my astonishment, in less than one minute I had landed my first trophy. It could have been a minnow for all I cared. Actually, it was not much larger. It was a five-inch "sunny," but I was as happy as if it had been a twelve-foot marlin. I was so excited that I just had to go share the good news with the rest of the clan. By this time, it was raining madly and Neal and I were sporting the typical rain garb of those days—yellow raincoats with matching "nerd"-style slicker hats. Running up the road, pole over the shoulder, I looked like a picture on a tuna can. As I burst into the front door of the cabin, I yelled for the family to come look at my prize. But as I did a Present Arms with my pole, my pride turned to shock. No fish! Looking down at my reel, I noticed that there was also no line! In all the excitement, I failed to notice that as I was running up the hill, my fish and line, caught in high brush, had remained down the hill. Now, I was forced to catch the fish again, but this time from the deck instead of the dock. By the time I got done rereeling the sunny back over the rocky path, the poor thing had a severe case of "road rash!" Nevertheless, I asked Dad to have the fish stuffed and mounted. After he stopped laughing I begged and pleaded, but it was to no avail. The fish was unceremoniously dumped in the garbage.

The next day, Dad surprised us by renting a motor boat. My mourning period for my sorry "sunny" had suddenly ended. The boat was a 1930'ish, wooden number, but to us, it was a luxury liner. Without a doubt, the little runabout made the vacation and brought us all closer together, (which is the only way five people could be on a twelve-foot boat. On the final day of our trip, we were informed that Mr. and Mrs. Barrett could henceforth be known as "Aunt Eleanor" and "Uncle Dick." I thought that the idea of having an optional aunt and uncle was a pretty good deal. The first fish, first boat ride and now, the first aunt and uncle of my choosing. All these "firsts" in just one week and in just one place. But more important, I had gone an entire week without having to look at people who were looking at me; without having to respond to the same boring inquiries about my face; without once hearing, "Hey, Crooked Mouth!"

FOUR

THE NOBLE HORSEMAN

Back in those early days, an unbridled imagination allowed me to slip in and out of reality with the greatest of ease. I hardly needed booze or drugs to accomplish the same thing. Yet, yearning to belong to my peer group, had it been offered, I probably would have indulged. Peer pressure was as strong then as it is today. It's a fact of life that spawns much of today's drug abuse and teenage suicides. For me however, being excluded from the so-called in-crowd, eventually worked to my advantage. Since no one ever offered me what was going around, succumbing to drug abuse was never a concern. As an added safeguard, my parents applied a unique approach to alcohol and drug abuse. In fact, considering it was back in the 1960s, their perspective on the matter was pretty radical. When I was fourteen, Dad caught me in the garage tossing down a cold one. Instead of punishing me, he sat me down and made the following statement, "If you want to drink or smoke, I won't stop you. My only stipulation is that you must do it in front of me." Well, permission was the last thing I wanted! I was a thrill-seeker and receiving permission had cheated me out of the thrill. It was a clear case of "the forbidden fruit is always sweeter." The psychology worked and henceforth my smoking, drug, and drinking pursuits remained nonexistent. Had he smacked me or simply ignored the incident as many parents do, I might not have fared so well. But I did not remain unscathed by peer pressure.

I'm willing to wager that one of you reading this story has a slightly crooked mouth, or walks with a bit of a limp, or is a little on the heavy side. You may have some affliction that sets you apart from the rest of your peer group. I was able to hide some of my own afflictions by blending in, losing myself in the crowd. But others who submit to peer pressure often lose themselves to the crowd. Just talk to those parents who have lost a child to booze or drugs. They'll probably tell you what they've told me on too many occasions, which is, "My child just wanted to be included; he (or she), wanted to belong."

We have all seen the symptoms of drug abuse and drunk driving. Tragically, the more subtle signs are often ignored or excused. Not until there is full-fledged addiction or death do we finally pay attention. By then it's frequently, and senselessly, too late. As I've said from the onset, the purpose of this story is to identify the cause of excessive substance abuse. Charles Dickens once wrote "Prevention is better than cure." It was true back in 1850 and it certainly applies today. Getting the drunk driver off the road after he or she has killed somebody is closing the barn door after the horse runs out. The cop in me arrests the drunk driver and thus treats the "symptom." The writer in me wants to "prevent" the tragedy by addressing the "cause."

Other than for the thrill of it and peer pressure, there is yet another cause of excessive drug and liquor abuse. This is the ever-present need for "escape." For millions of people seeking relief from life's unavoidable pressures and pains, drugs and alcohol become the vehicle of escape. As you have seen, a highly imaginative mind was my vehicle of escape, and daydreams and illusions were constant companions. I had more ways to escape than Harry Houdini! After a while, the ploys I used to remove myself from reality became as intoxicating and addictive as any drug.

Escapists constitute a very large and fraternal organization. But escapism resolves nothing and only delays the inevitable. I intend to demonstrate, in this chapter and the next, that there is no escape from oneself. But I'm going to let questions of others dictate the direction of the message. One of my lectures given to the PTA was recorded on videotape. The excerpts of the session were transcribed into this chapter.

Q.: Officer Waimon, you—"Excuse me, please call me Larry." Okay, Larry. You just got done telling us that there is no such thing as "paradise," or more specifically, no escape from oneself. Yet, hearing you speak about those early days in Lake George, it sounds like you were desperately looking for just that, some kind of escape, or paradise or something. So what exactly *did* you find there?

A.: What I found was an oasis, a temporary reprieve from life's problems. As I mentioned before, nobody knew me there. No one asked the usual question about my crooked mouth. I was

53

allowed to feel "normal" and I thoroughly enjoyed being anonymous, an ordinary face in the crowd. I caught my first fish there, I water-skied for the first time, it was the very first time our family had ever spent a whole week together. All in all, it was just a great bunch of "firsts." I immediately started to associate Lake George with something good in my life, something pleasurable. The experience was intoxicating and once home, once back in reality, I kept trying to relive the good memories over and over again. As soon as I felt the familiar pressures, instead of facing them, I'd allow my imagination to transfer me back up to the lake, back where I felt secure and insulated. By the following summer, Lake George became more than just a place to vacation. What it represented was my own little haven of retreat, a fortress; a place where I could effectively block out life's unpleasantries. You know now that I think about it, I was playing an unfortunate game of tag. Back home in the real world, I felt vulnerable. I could be hurt, I was "it." Lake George represented "home base" and nothing or no one could harm me, I couldn't be tagged.

Now compare this experience to someone who does drugs or alcohol for the very first time. If this first encounter is a pleasant one, naturally this individual is inclined to repeat the sensation. Too many "repeat sensations" however, and that person runs the risks of dependency and addiction. Subsequently, the priorities of the user start to change dramatically. Being "high" becomes the only reality this person is concerned with. "Getting there" becomes a full-time pursuit that often excludes everything and everyone else. I too had become emotionally addicted to escape, and inasmuch that the end justifies the means, I was willing to make a lot of senseless trade-offs.

Q.: "Can you tell this group what those trade-offs were?"

A.: All too vividly. Think back to the last time you really tied one on. Did anybody approach you the day after your "high" and say "Boy, last night you were the life of the party!" Have you ever replied with a polite smile having no recollection of what the hell they're talking about? All too often when we are that "buzzed" the recollection of what happened during that high diminishes as we start the reality, the "trade-off" that *always* lasts a heck of a lot longer than the so-called high.

Does the word "hangover" strike a familiar note? (The audience responds with knowing laughter.) Somehow, we always seem to pay a price for our good times.

For me, every day spent away from my home town was a good day. Lake George was an emancipation from my usual problems and thus, in itself, it became my "high." Returning home was a total bummer and my concerns would immediately turn to next year's getaway. The fifty weeks between these excursions were virtually surrendered to wishing life away—a write-off! Placing so much emphasis on just two weeks out of the year kind of makes one wonder whatever happened to the other fifty. Think of it as a two-week high followed by a fifty-week hangover! Like the drug abuser, I forsook reality for unreality. For too many years, I grew older but I never grew up. The trade-off for my illusions was a lot of wasted time. I paid dearly for those two weeks out of the year.

Q.: It seems as though you were your own worst enemy and that your vacations did you more harm than good. I compliment you for being able to admit your shortcomings; I don't know if I could be as up-front as you are being about my own faults. Did anything good ever really come out of those trips to the Adirondacks?

A.: Well, that's a comment and question; I'll try to address them both. First of all, thanks for the compliment. As far as being able and willing to admit my faults, well, let me say this: As long as I recognize that a problem exists, I'm usually good at admitting it. After all, when you've made a colossal ass of yourself, the best thing to do is to "fess up," cut your losses, and start again. I was always self-critical and often poked fun at myself before my peers had a chance to. I suppose it was a case of "you can't fire me, I quit"; beat them to the punch and save your dignity. But the bottom line here is this. I'm trying to make a point. I'm hoping to demonstrate just how counterproductive drugs and other excesses really are. If debasing myself helps to convey this point, then so be it. I promised you the truth, even if it's to the exclusion of pride and vanity.

As far as your question is concerned, the answer is a resounding "yes," a lot of good did come out of those trips up north. Separating fact from fiction, the fact was that our family grew a lot closer because of those vacations. Before Lake George, we had no special family activity. With a thirty-two mile crystal-clear lake, it was appropriate, if not inevitable, that we got involved with boating. Dad loved it because it was an excuse to be together. I couldn't water-ski unless he drove the boat and vice versa. Boats quickly became a passion and one of the few indulgences my father allowed himself. Over the next twenty-three years, Dad found an excuse to purchase twenty-three boats. Every season, they got slightly bigger and a bit faster. We had names for all those boats but we never kept them long enough to put those names on! But there was method to what seemed like utter madness. My father had found an interest that the entire family could be involved with. By selling the boats at the end of every summer, he spawned an off-season family project, which was researching next year's purchase. Dad would swear that he couldn't make the selection without *all* our input. He supplemented this looking with extended boating courses sponsored by the United States Power Squadron. Before each test he would have me grill him on possible test questions. Once again, it was a ploy to keep us involved as a family. With or without help, he always got perfect scores and piloted a boat with the same finesse that he once used to pilot a stunt plane. But I'll tell you what gave me the biggest kick. Most of the year my father was Mr. Businessman. He was extremely capable, hard-working, and much of the time, quite serious—almost stuffy. But come the day we would leave for the lake, he would go through some kind of metamorphosis. My straight-and-narrow father would snap out of bed at 5:00 A.M. and signal the start of the vacation. With some highly uncharacteristic moves, Dad would go tearing through the house in his pajamas and whistle like a ship's boatswain piping the troops aboard. Then he would shout at the top of his voice, "Boats leaving! Boats leaving!" He carried on like this every year; it became a tradition. We all got a kick seeing him so out of character and so genuinely happy.

Now, I'm not saying that family involvement and loving parents guarantees that your kids will grow up drug- and problem-free. I'm merely suggesting that you consider some of the causes of peer pressure—a need to belong, a desire to be included. Perhaps if more children found some of those essentials in their own home, they might be less inclined to search for dangerous substitutes elsewhere.

Q.: Larry, reality dictates that there really is no such thing as Shangri-la. When did you finally realize that Lake George, as much as you honestly loved the place, was no garden of Eden?

A.: Now, there's a good question, and as a matter of fact, I've got a good answer. I realized there was no garden of Eden as soon as I started searching for an Eve. The owners of the Gate House had a daughter; her name was Susan. She was an attractive blonde, blue-eyed fourteen-year-old, and quite buxom for her age—all in all, a perfect candidate for a first crush. For an entire vacation, I ran after that girl and she did some running too. Unfortunately, it was always in the opposite direction! It was a bit of a setback but my ego was rebuilt the following year when I met a new love interest and once again, there were more good "firsts." But the notion of a Shangri-la really came under fire just a few years later. The owners of the resort both succumbed to illness and died. Mike and Blanche Cotherman *were* the Gate House. We regarded them as family and I truly loved those two hard-working people. Other than for the death of a great-grandmother and President Kennedy, I had never experienced such a loss; I was devastated. The Gate House was never the same again. It was then that I concluded that it was the *people* that made that place what it was; not a lake, or the pine trees, or the boats. Soon thereafter, we had our own lakehouse built, but things felt different without the Gate House and the Cothermans. I finally saw that paradise was indeed flawed.

Q.: It sounds like your priorities in life were being reassessed. Did reality finally start to shape your life?

A.: Look, let me be honest with you. Unreality can take on as many different forms as there are drugs to get you there. As you have seen, I used imagination the way others use drugs and alcohol. I'm sure that you have also concluded that I had an arsenal of illusions at my disposal. When one fantasy was no longer available, I would simply acquire another. In 1963 my folks took me to see *Mutiny on the Bounty*, starring

Marlon Brando and Trevor Howard. I was totally enchanted by MGM's version of the Tahiti of yesteryear. Suddenly, the lure of Lake George was dwarfed by a new fantasy, a new paradise to seek out. Seven years later, I climbed aboard a DC-8 and winged my way to that fabled island in search of God-knows-what. Having the dream just wasn't enough; I was in the business of making all those dreams come true! Well, maybe I'd better elaborate on that. Like most kids who grew up on the 1950s and '60s, I was greatly influenced by what I saw on T.V. The hero-type characters, whether real or imaginary, became the role models that I would try and pattern myself after. They were my alter ego, something to supplement what was missing from my own personality—inner strength, security, self-confidence. I adored the power figure and the fact that might always made right. Of course, my heroes were always on the side of right and therefore, always the mightiest! But when I concluded that jumping over buildings in a single bound was totally out of the question, I switched my allegiance over to yet another mythical character.

Hercules, or more accurately, the gentleman who played him, Steve Reeves, now here was a guy who was worthy of my consideration. He couldn't walk on water and he couldn't fly through the air. So in my deluded way of thinking, this character had more credibility than the others who preceded him. Then I started thinking, gee, if I only had a body like that, who would dare call me "Crooked Mouth" again, or for that matter, anything else short of "Sir!" Here, I thought, was the answer to all my problems. I couldn't control the symmetry of my smile, but I could definitely control the circumference of my biceps. Body building became instant gratification and within no time flat I was having myself a banner year in the recognition department. For the most part however, it seemed to be the teeny-boppers and lonely housewives who paid me the most mind. Nevertheless, any attention was welcomed and it was a good kick in the ego, a long time in coming. So naturally, I figured that if a little was good, more was better. Developing my body quickly became more paramount than improving the "gray matter." So after I had quit my third college, I applied my physical prowess where I thought it would do the most good and enlisted in the Army Airborne. It was during the height of the Viet Nam War and I don't mind telling you, I was drawn to the military for all the wrong reasons; I'll spare you the details. Remarkably however, an alert army doctor remedied the situation just three months later. During a routine exam, he noticed that my left eye wouldn't quite close due to my childhood paralysis. He gave me a long speech on how the army couldn't be responsible for further injury to the eye. Things could blow up in my face and I wouldn't be able to blink and protect that eye; this was the example he used. That day, I was sent home with an honorable discharge in my hand and a tear in my eye. In retrospect however, in light of the war, the accident that had plagued me all my life may have indeed been responsible for *saving* my life! It's a bit of irony that I think about from time to time, though back then I did not have the luxury of this hindsight. Being invited to leave the army was regarded as yet another blow to my self-esteem.

Fortunately for me, back in the '60s, it was fashionable not to know where your head was at, so I was very much in fashion! For some strange reason, I thought at the time that there was indeed escape from oneself and that my bruised ego *could* be healed by running away. So I ran, all across the country; always searching for what I don't know. This odyssey landed me, appropriately enough, in the place known as the "City of Lost Souls," Las Vegas, Nevada. Once there, I got a job managing a health spa, modeled bathing suits at the Sands Hotel, and worked part time for a very discreet male escort service. I returned home with little more than an overhauled, if not overinflated ego; again, brawn had prevailed over brain.

Q.: Larry, I always thought that people who became policemen were kind of straight and conventional. Your past life sounds like some kind of adventure story and at the very least, far from conventional. How did you ever become a policeman!

A.: I expected this one. However, the question should be rephrased as "why" instead of "how." The reasons I became a cop were both typical and idealistic. Perhaps it was the promise of adventure, or maybe it was the fact that I wouldn't either have to work a nine-to-five job or be stuck in an office; maybe that was it. At least, these are some of the more typical reasons. But here's a more compelling and honest reason: I'm, or at least I was, an incorrigible idealist. I thought that when I put on that police uniform, a lot of wrongs were going to be righted and that "truth, justice, and the American way" were finally going to prevail. I thought I was going to make a difference. I tried to champion so many causes that one of my fellow officers, Tom Lombardi, gave me the nickname "Crusader Rabbit," a childhood cartoon hero of mine. A more appropriate comparison would have been that old windmill chaser, Don Quixote. Suffice it to say, what I was looking for was simply never found and I'll leave it at that. Just consider this—think about the reason for me being here today and the tragedies our family has sustained over the last four decades. The so-called "system" couldn't prevent what happened. The "system" wouldn't supply a punishment to fit the crime. I am *part* of that system. Isn't that ironic? Now that I think about it, the question should not have been— "How did you" or even "Why did you become a policeman?" The real questions here are—why do I continue to serve a system that refuses to serve me? Who protects the protector?

Q.: Larry, I'm a clinical psychiatrist. You seem to have spent a great deal of time fulfilling fantasies that most of us merely dream about. Speaking for all of us, we've appreciated your honesty and frankness; it's been very enlightening. As parents, we often forget what it was like growing up under the thumb of peer influence and related pressures. This discussion has jolted our memories and perhaps henceforth, we'll all be a little more attentive to our children's needs and apprehensions.

What disturbs me however, is the fact that you are too self-critical. You mentioned that you didn't live in the "real world" and that you "wasted a lot of time." The only thing different about your shortcomings and many of our own is the fact that you were willing to admit them! This puts you miles ahead of a lot of other people who still maintain the notion that paradise *does* exist. It puts you very much in focus *with* reality. If there was one thing that did it for you, one thing that brought you to your senses, what might that one thing be?

A.: This time it's "who" instead of "what." But first let me thank you for your comments. I believe I detected a compliment, which my fragile ego appreciates. Anyway, in answer to your question: a gentleman lived on the street directly behind our home in Livingston called Nathanial Christopher Weiss (Nat.) He purchased the home because it included one of the last remaining stables that existed in our town. Mr. Weiss kept his horse there. Lady Calhoun was a magnificent and highly spirited English thoroughbred. The neighbor's son who had been taking care of Lady was going off to college and Nat had asked him to find a suitable replacement. I was approached first and accepted the position without hesitation, especially since it meant that I could ride as often as I wished. "Bonanza" was my favorite T.V. show at the time; this was like having my private Ponderosa right in my own backyard.

But more spirited than the horse itself was that mare's owner, Nat. He looked like the leading man from some romantic adventure yarn. At 6 feet 2 inches, Nat cut a very imposing figure, and he had this deep, groundshaking voice that registered about nine on the Richter scale. But by no means was this gentleman all talk. Helping to settle any altercation that should arise, were two well-trained fists, a byproduct of his boyhood days as a ranked amateur boxer. All in all, he was not the kind of guy you would want to annoy. He didn't walk softly and he certainly didn't need a big stick. Once during my many visits, Mr. Weiss noticed two very large prowlers staring through the window. He leaped from his seat and gave chase. Nat caught the two; it wasn't a pretty sight. Even a ride to the store could, without a moment's notice, turn into a wild adventure—actually, a misadventure if you were the unfortunate soul who cut him off or were guilty of riding on his tail. Road menaces were dealt a unique brand of curbside justice.

Now if all this sounds like a serious case of idol worship, it would indeed be an accurate assessment. At age 16, I was certainly in the market for a role model. Remember, like some of your own children, I was desperately looking to supplement the void caused by the lack of friendships and self-esteem. Of course, who needed friends when John Wayne resided right in your own backyard! I hung out with Mr. Weiss at every opportunity and my biggest thrill came when I was given permission to call him Nat. I mean, really, how many people get to call their heroes by their first name?

Not everyone however, shared my enthusiasm for our special friendship. Probably not his two daughters and cer-

The "noble horseman." Nat and Lady

tainly not his wife; I capitalized on too much of their family time and constantly interfered. But the one I hurt the most was my father. After every thrilling exploit with the great Nat Weiss, I'd run on home to report the exciting details to my dad. All the chatter over my neighbor tended to undermine a great father/son relationship. He found it increasingly difficult to compete with a living legend. Eventually, however, Dad quietly thanked Nat for what he was able to accomplish with me.

You see, Nat had a mind that was just as sharp as his left hook. It was his brains, not his brawn, that had turned his self-made business into a huge success. Nat also had acquired a great deal of wisdom, which he applied on me regularly. For my benefit, he removed himself from the pedestal that I had placed him on. He began by recounting some of his own past; a childhood often punctuated with loneliness and ridicule. I found that hard to believe but then he told me why. For some strange reason his mother saw fit to make him look pretty instead of handsome. She dressed him in frilly, almost feminine outfits and styled his hair like Prince Valiant. He was as much of an outcast from his peer group as I had been from mine and fought for very much the same reasons. Suddenly, Nat had established credibility as a mere mortal and I was receptive to hearing more. He insisted that his fighting ways should neither be admired or mimicked, that in fact on too many occasions he had made a "spectacle" of himself as a result of his temper. Nat asserted that "he who throws the first punch admits to losing the battle," and followed up the quote by suggesting that I start living my own life. He told me to stop hiding behind the muscles and false bravado, to stop borrowing a personality from some Hollywood script. Nat continued by telling me to always be myself, the only thing real friends would expect *and* accept from me. Actually, what he said was "You can't expect others to like you if you don't first like yourself, so cut the crap!" Our fireside chat ended with yet another quote, this one from a renowned poet. "Man is really three men. He is the man he thinks he is, the man others think he is, and he's the man he *really* is." Nat said that unless I could accept what I *really* am, I could waste a lifetime searching elsewhere for an identity that was within me all along.

Mr. Nathaniel Weiss, this "noble horseman," has provided us all with a moral to this story.

Q.: Larry, you're very fortunate to have had such a friend as Mr. Weiss; I wish there was someone like him around when I was growing up. Now, would you indulge us by answering just one last question and tell all the men in this room what Tahiti was *really* like?

A.: That involves the Tahiti syndrome....

FIVE

THE TAHITI SYNDROME

Time to make a point: If your only desire is to "arrive," then the mode of transportation is inconsequential. Being there is everything; how you got there means nothing. When we seek escape from life's pressures, relief is all that matters and not the vehicle that brings it. For some, that "vehicle" might be a toke, a line of coke, or dealer's choice. For others, it could be a drink or two, or seven or eight.

As I've discussed, I too sought escape from life's pressures and did so quite often. But in those earlier days, a vivid and wondrous imagination was all that was necessary. Escaping into fantasy land was how I spelled relief, and my techniques of getting there were finely honed. Back then, the booze and drugs never concerned me. Ironically, since I was excluded from my peer group, peer pressure to drink and toke never really entered the picture. Nevertheless, the constant search for Shangri-la became as addictive and intoxicating as any other bad habit.

Daydreams don't destroy brain cells or waste away your liver. But like even the most hardcore addiction, my dependency on illusions was wasting something just as precious as any body part. What it had wasted was my time, and like the use of your liver, once it's gone, it never comes back. To make my point, I'll have to try something a lot more radical than tough talk. I'm going to try reason by example.

Everybody that does drugs is looking for something; I was looking for something—relief, escape, utopia. It illustrates unhappiness or dissatisfaction with what's going on right now, today. The "trip" offers us a place to hide, a momentary sanctuary from life's oppressions. But our relief is fleeting, lasting for only as long as the drug will sustain us. The need to hide from our problems starts the vicious cycle all over again, and soon, before we know it, we're hooked.

At every presentation, I challenge my audience with the same dare. I first submit to them that, yes, being high does indeed feel good. "But," I tell them, "I defy just one of you to stand up and tell me that coke, or grass or booze has in fact cured your problems." No one ever has, no one ever will. All the drug use ever does is to forestall the inevitable. It resolves nothing. When you finally realize that, you'll probably wonder as I did: "In my unending quest for a better tomorrow, just how many good todays have I actually given up?" My story serves as a vivid example of wasted time.

If you were thoroughly convinced that what you are seeking simply doesn't exist, you would stop looking for it. The specifics of your illusion don't matter, fantasy is fantasy. "Fantasy" and "paradise" are notions that exist in the mind only. Not only did I fantasize about the garden of Eden, I spent all my money and had traveled 7,600 miles traveling to Tahiti actually looking for it! By the time the journey was over, I had realized that what was sought simply didn't exist and things started to turn around for me. Finally, my life started to have some perspective.

By sharing this adventure with you, perhaps you will draw the same conclusions that I have. Maybe then, you too will enjoy a new perspective on your own life. Maybe then, some of you will get on with your lives, in the *real* world.

The following account has been taken from my original journal kept during my trip to Tahiti.

Well, I can hardly believe it; I'm actually on my way! I've studied the customs and culture of French Polynesia for over six years. I've read all three books of the Bounty trilogy, learned to sing their songs. I know how to dance their dance. But what do I really know about "today's" Tahiti? Like many people, I am a latent hedonist, devoted to the pleasures of life. But will I find Tahiti to be, as Captain Bligh once put it, "the finest island in the world," or would it be just a colossal bursted bubble? It's time to stop wondering—time to trade the gun and badge for the flowered *lei* and loincloth. Time to go from cop to "cop-out". The anticipation is overwhelming.

Friday, Sept. 18, 1970
Flight 19 United Airlines
Take-off time 12:10 P.M.
Entry #1 2:20 P.M.
Welcome to the "Friendly Skies of United." Just finished a fine lunch of steak and king crab and am feeling great! Peter Bartsch,

my German traveling companion who I bamboozled into going with me, is telling third-grade caliber jokes, but they're making time pass. Enthusiasm at this point is somewhat less than I had anticipated. Perhaps, this is due to not reconciling the fact that after all these years, I'm actually on my way. I expect an attitude change on the final leg of the flight.

Entry #2   Sept. 19   9:03 A.M.

After an agonizing eight-hour layover in L.A. Airport, we're airborne once again. Next stop Faaa Airport, Tahiti. Outside of drinking, which I'm not too good at, there is virtually nothing to do at that terminal. Downtown L.A. was too far out of the way and after about four hours, you start counting the tiles in the men's room for entertainment. Well, that's all behind us now and my spirits are finally up to par with the altitude. Take-off was at 11:53 P.M. according to my faithful chronograph, and what a white-knuckle take-off it was; we must have used up every inch of runway to get this DC-8 off the ground. There is a full complement of about 130 passengers on board (apparently my quest for utopia is not very original.) What a crowd this is I might add; I don't think that there is anybody, save for this girl sitting next to me, under fifty. Judging from the passive expressions on their faces, they just don't epitomize vitality and enthusiasm.

Entry #3   Sept. 19   9:10 P.M.

Well, here I am in my own thatched hut courtesy of Club Mediteranée, so dead to the world that I'm all but lying in state! In a word, the trip over can only be described as grueling. The five-and-one-half hour flight from New Jersey to L.A., the eight-hour layover, another eight-hour flight to Faaa Airport aboard a crowded DC-8, all were bad enough. Then the real fun begins: From Faaa, they take you on "Le Truck," AKA the "Wooden Cadillac," a 1920 open freight bus, to Tahiti's capital, Papeete. We then boarded a boat, appropriately called the "Liki Tiki," for the seven mile trip to Moorea, our island. The jaunt turned out to be an ordeal. The water is quite tranquil until you clear the lagoon. It then becomes extremely turbulent. It was not the kind of choppiness I had been used to on lakes, a most disturbing pitch and roll that's guaranteed to make the hardiest of souls a bit queasy. I suppose that it was from lack of sleep and so little to eat caused by my exuberance that put me in a rundown condition. This, compounded by shooting film near the boat's exhaust through the tiny viewfinder and simultaneously trying to maintain my equilibrium made me terribly ill. My lips started to tingle and I broke out in a cold sweat. My tan suddenly vanished and I turned ghost-white. Then I got that helpless feeling like my innards were going to spew out from both ends at the same time. Helplessly, I walked over to the captain and with explicit sign language and some very pathetic gestures, I asked him where the ship's "head" was. With a toothy grin, he pointed down towards the bilge. On my arrival, headfirst, I might add (I slipped on a coconut shell), I witnessed a sight that threw me into sheer panic. There was only one toilet and there were at least ten people ahead of me! Well, if misery loves company, I certainly had much to love aboard the "Liki Tiki." Dragging myself toward the aft of the boat, I tried to make some on-the-spot deals with the Lord or the devil, whoever came first, to relinquish me from my present state of affairs. In return I was promising to give up the entire trip, go back where I came from. At one point I was even hoping that a hungry shark or King Neptune would appear to put me out of my misery! Nothing materialized and my situation became desperate! But then the miracle on the Forty-second Parallel occurred. The boat stopped rocking! We had finally entered Moorea's lagoon. Turning to face the island, I was filled with such awe that my symptoms almost completely subsided. We had passed through the barrier reef and the water had changed from deep blue to turquoise and had become extremely serene. I immediately recognized one of the twin volcanic peaks as Bali Hai Mountain. It rose dramatically from the sea and pierced through a magnificent cloud formation, making it look as though the volcano was still active. We circled past the twin bays, Pao Pao (Cook Bay) and Opunohu Bay and were about to dock the boat in a cove. When we reached the northwest side of the island, there to greet us in loincloths and ukeleles were a few of the local islanders who serenaded us onto another one of those open freight trucks. At long last, we arrived at the Club's village, where we were greeted by "vahines," who placed flowered wreaths atop our heads and kissed us on both cheeks, the traditional Tahitian welcome.

Our social director, Mike, is a real piece of work: he sympathized with our miserable trip and his hilarious orientation speech made everyone feel easy. Mike stands about five foot two, has large mutton chops but no hair on his head. His belly plummets over his ankle-length loincloth and he tops off his impeccable appearance with a gigantic straw hat covered with real pieces of fruit. He looks like the male counterpart to "Chiquita Banana!"

After a ceremonial drink, we were escorted to our living quarters, or "fare," meaning house, but which can only be described as a thatch-roofed A-frame. Inside, it's quite simple but very attractive and it even has modern plumbing in the bathroom!

After a little exploring, I discovered the Club's boutique and in no time flat, I was donning my very own loincloth, called a "pareu" by the Tahitians. If my brother officers could only see me now! Clad in nothing more than a pareu, a smile, and a flowered wreath, they'd have me pegged as some kind of Anglo-Polynesian transvestite.

Entry #4   Sept. 20   9:30 A.M.
Good morning, and welcome to "Wild Kingdom!" Spent an uneasy night listening to wild critters scampering across our thatched roof. It turned out to be lizards, which are quite harmless. However, I couldn't convince Peter of that and he insisted (at 3:00 A.M.) that I walk around his bed and tuck the mosquito netting into the edges of the mattress. My final trip to the bathroom that night was interrupted when, from out of nowhere, this flying creature circled my head and landed right in the sink. It looked like a miniature "Rodan," and shocked me so badly that I finished urinating everywhere but in the bowl! I very gingerly walked over to the sink, only to find a giant roach that appeared to be a good four inches long from stem to stern. But he wasn't alone; some of his compadres decided to crawl up from the plumbing for a late night rendezvous. It looked like the annual cockroach convention! I promptly turned on the hot water and all but the original ringleader quickly dispersed. He winged his way to higher ground. Because of his tenacity, I gave him the pet name "Leo de-Roacha." But Leo's stay proved to be very short-lived. This morning a large lizard, our only pesticide, had just about totally consumed poor Leo, leaving just his head hanging out of the lizard's mouth, its antennae still waving goodbye. So much for "Adventures in Paradise."

Lunch and dinner yesterday were real feasts. Although the accommodations are relatively simple, the meals are extremely lavish. This seems to be a direct result of the French influence, which is very evident around the club. Lunch is a buffet-type affair with at least thirty varieties of French-Polynesian food, and you can gorge yourself at every meal. Meals are everything but hurried. I'm just not used to taking two hours to eat, but here they wouldn't have it any other way, another European overtone. Dinners are slightly different. They are served family-style in groups of eight to a table. The person who is unlucky enough to sit at the head of the table has to pass around and serve every course of the meal to all the individuals at the table. Tonight, I'll make sure not to sit at the head of the table!

After dinner, everybody went to the bar for the night's festivities. It was there I decided that the term "natural rhythm," should really be applied to the Tahitians. Their musical talents are a class by themselves. But then they started the fast hip-shaking dance called the "tamure," and the vahines set into motion everything from the waist down at blinding speed. No wonder they call this the mating dance! The music paused briefly, and then started up again. It didn't seem possible, but this time the tamure was being played even faster and everybody in the room, regardless of age, kept beat to the music or danced as if they were in some kind of hypnotic trance. When I couldn't stand it anymore, I popped up out of my chair, slid in between two vahines who were dancing by themselves and then proceeded to try my hand (or shall I say my hip) at the tamure. I had waited six years for this dance, and my heart was pounding as fast as the drums. I was so overwhelmed by the whole experience that when I tried to dance, my legs got rubbery and I fell right on my ass! I got up and "tamured" myself right out of the bar in embarrassment.

Soon, Pete and I decided that we had had enough excitement for one night so we started back to our little hut. When we saw the first row of "fares," we started to get nervous. All 150 huts are mirror images of each other, and it's almost impossible to locate the right one even in broad daylight. At night, if you can locate your hut within an hour, it's considered a small miracle! When they told us that the natives who numbered the huts were drunk at the time, I thought they were kidding. But the joke was on us as we wandered aimlessly from fare to fare. There are no locks on the doors, and we apologized over and over again in French and English for several invasions of privacy before finally locating our beds.

Entry #5   Sept. 21   11:30 P.M.
"Paradise" has produced a few casualties today. A German film crew is down here, filming some kind of serial on our island.

Welcome to Paradise

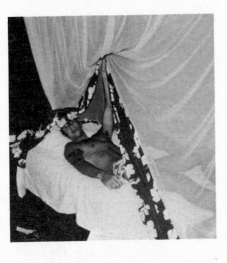

Which house is mine?

Fantasy, 1970

Reality, with Bonnie, 1983

WHEN TEARS DON'T WORK

During the shooting, the poor camera man discovered the "secret of coconut oil" when he was struck on the head by a falling coconut. They took him to Tahiti's hospital for treatment of concussion. I've decided not to take any more siestas under palm trees.

The next mishap occurred to a woman who no one could stand anyway—one of those pseudo-sophisticates who finds fault with everything and everybody and believes she can walk on water. Well, today she failed in her attempt to walk on water and fell right on her "barrier reef," cutting her backside on some fire coral! I noticed that she stood throughout dinner tonight.

Calamity even struck my poor friend Peter. His light German skin is hardly the most desirable near or about the equator—witness his second-degree sunburn. Tonight, the pain in his legs got so intense that I was forced to render makeshift first aid. I smeared Noxema all over the back and front of his legs, threw a rope over the rafter above his bed, tied his ankles together, and hoisted his legs off the bed to offer him some relief. The sight of Peter's agony was so pathetic that it reminded me of Job enduring all his plagues simultaneously!

The day was not without some consolation. We watched a soccer game played on an improvised field. Tahitian and American sports are similar in some ways. As in the U.S., there is a refreshment stand, but instead of the concessionaire reaching in his cooler and pulling out a Pepsi and a bottle opener, he reaches into his wicker chest, pulls out a nice cool coconut, and pops the top off it with three quick whacks from his machete. Rather than the traditional hamburger and hot dog routine, vendors offer Tahitian-style kabob served on a long skewer. The fans, though, (not the players) were the real entertainment. Instead of cheering or booing their respective teams, they laugh at them! The team captain fell down, giving up the ball to the opposite team, who immediately scored an easy goal. The captain who fell twisted his ankle, and the fans laughed. Tahitians just love to laugh. Their main phrase is "Aita pea' pea,"—"It does not matter' or "Nothing really matters."—an enlightening observation and it sums up their way of life.

A strange thing—I've only been here a few days and already I miss my fiancée, Janice, so much that I've seriously thought of leaving early. In fact, today I went to the club's main office to ask about an end-of-the-week flight, but there isn't one.

So here I lie, watching two lizards on the ceiling who appear to be doing the tamure and thinking how I seem to be destined to enjoy "paradise" whether I want to or not.

Entry #6   Sept. 22   Tuesday night
Today, Peter and I took Billy's circle tour of the island. Billy is one of the most enterprising islanders I've come across so far. In his little open-window bus, he took us on a fascinating jaunt around Moorea. The tour mainly consisted of stopping off at all of Billy's relatives' homes. Now, there are only four thousand people on the entire island, and I bet that one thousand of them are directly related to Billy! It was far from boring, though. The first stop on the agenda was Billy's house, where we met his family and got our first real taste of Polynesian customs and culture. His eighteen-month-old daugher did the tamure for us, and I got the impression that the Tahitians are endowed with fluid rhythm at a very young age; she was adorable. Then Billy almost literally walked straight up a palm tree to pick us some coconuts. Boy, could I get this guy a lineman's job for Bell Tel! He then gave us a live demonstration in the art of husking and cracking a coconut. Billy made it look so easy that I just had to try it myself. I took his machete and, after much perseverance, managed to husk and crack the nut but spilled all the milk on my foot in the process! I then noticed blood trickling down my hand. In my exuberance, I had done a better job of husking my hand than the lousy coconut!

From there, we rambled along Moorea's only road, stopping off to visit more of Billy's kin, gathering mangos, papayas, and other epicurean delights for our picnic lunch. The midday feast took place in a beautiful lagoon on the white sand beach. Billy and I started a fire with some coconut husks and we placed breadfruit right into the blaze. Breadfruit, called "Uru" by the natives, was Captain Bligh's sole purpose for his Bounty expedition. It was to be gathered up and used as a cheap food staple to feed the slaves in British-owned colonies. Of course, I was anxious to try this fruit, which was responsible for that famous mutiny. I tasted the cooked paste. Except for the flavor of the butter we dipped it in, it was very bland. I think the lack of really chewy food and calcium in their diet accounts for the poor condition of the island-ers' teeth and skin.

We then went to a famous historical site located on the north side of the island, the ancient sacrificial alta called "Ti Ti Aroa," or "Woman with the Great Breasts." Folklore has it that the pagans, about two centuries ago, sacrificed a very well-endowed woman here and named the altar after her renowned features. As we stood among the lush flora, ankle-deep in mud, the mood of "sacrifice" was literally in the air. Swarms of the most formidable mosquitos were eating us alive and Billy's broken English dissertation about the big-breasted woman was quickly aborted. As we all fled to less carnivorous turf, I turned to Peter with the musical question, "If these are mosquitos, can this be paradise?"

Before long, we were back on the bus, scratching our way to the next port of call. Billy passed around some limes to put on our bites. The acidic juice from that remarkable fruit seems to be a cure-all for every kind of skin irritation. The resourcefulness of the Tahitians never fails to astound me. Soon we arrived at our final stop, Bali Hai Hotel. It's one of the most successful operations in the area, started by three Americans who came to this island to "escape" the drudgeries of their professions. Ironically enough, it's rumored that one of the partners has developed a full-fledged ulcer, and it's a fact that all three work their asses off!

We left the hotel after a brief tour and were back on the road (and I use that word loosely), for our quick stop at the island's main bays, Pao Pao and Opunohu. Those particular spots on the island were soothing to the soul. The twin lagoons are quietly nestled among the tall palms with Bali Hai Mountain rising from water's edge; it's breathtaking!

Entry #7   Sept. 23   Wednesday afternoon
The natives are restless! I just got chased off the nude beach by some pretty irate vahines. They had no qualms about running completely bare-assed, but they certainly objected to me filming them and one of them said something to me in Tahitian (I'm sure it wasn't "Happy Birthday"), and then to add insult to injury, she kicked sand in my face.

Now I'm sitting in front of my "fare"watching a huge land crab diligently working to finish his home in the ground. These crabs seem to be all over the island and last night I saw them put to good use—crab-racing night, Tahitian style.

Entry #8   Sept. 29   Thursday night
Today, we took the inevitable excursion to the main island of Tahiti. The trip over was certainly less traumatic than that "Liki

74

Tiki" jaunt. We flew from Moorea on a plane called a "Twin Ot-ter," and we were perfectly willing to take our chances with the student pilot rather than to endure that intolerable boat ride.

Upon reaching Papeete, the capital, I found myself in a very bustling town. This was in sharp contrast to the subdued atmos-phere on Moorea. The Tahitians' workday includes a three-hour afternoon siesta, but at least they make a token effort to work. In Moorea, it seems that the women do most of the chores around and about the club, but no one seems to work very hard or very long. Our first stop just had to be Quinn's Bar, the most noto-rious bar in the South Pacific. So many accounts have been given about this historical landmark, but the one that is the most apt has to be quoted from the July issue of Skin Diver magazine: "But at first glance this large, rambling, broken-down sort of build-ing, largely open on to the street is disappointing. You can see the bamboo letters spelling out "Quinns" across the facade. You wait for something to happen—and usually something does happen. (For example a body comes flying out the door and lands at your feet on the pavement). So you go in—or rather you try to go in, beating your way through the stacks of floral dresses, striped sailor jerseys, heaving breasts, menacing biceps, stale breath, peeling make-up, stinking mops of rancid oily hair, drunken hiccups, pools of beer, toothy grins, down-at-the-heel girls, nightmarish female impersonators, flabbergasted tourists, blasé papas, lingering typists—all to the accompaniment of the infor-mal uproar thumbed out by an epileptic orchestra, which no-body pays attention to. . . . " This is what lured us to that reputed place, but because it was morning very little activity was taking place. However, I did make one startling discovery; the toilets were all coed! In fact, all the privies in Tahiti are strictly of the "he-she" type.

Back outside the bar, we were approached by a Chinese gent who talked us into taking a tour of the island in this 1969 Ford. The guide spoke four languages and the car ride, instead of a crowded bus, certainly made the tour more tolerable. About a mile out of the city limits, it grew peaceful again. Tahiti, like Moorea, is not inhabited in the interior of the island. They say old superstitions and taboos are responsible for this. People believe there are ghosts on Moorea. Unlike its sister island, however there is no barrier reef to protect Tahiti from the battering waves. This condition has produces several spectacular blowholes and rock formations. The beauty of the island chain is endless—

unfortunately, the sight of T.V. antennas poking out the top of several thatched huts, along with several construction sites, makes this island less attractive than Moorea.

At long last I found myself standing by the lighthouse at Point Venus. This is where Captain Cook observed the first transit of Venus across the sun. I walked a few more feet onto the beach and found myself standing in the exact spot where Captains Wallis, Cook, and Bligh first set foot on Tahiti's shores. That eerie "George Washington slept here" feeling suddenly came over me, and I must have stood motionless for at least ten minutes just taking it all in. Moving on, we came to Tahiti's botanical gardens with its indescribably beautiful island flowers. The Gauguin Museum was our next stop, but I chose not to go in. Though I've always been fascinated by this artist's tragic life, I never relished his works. So while I waited for Peter, I took a stroll to the black sand beach. Here volcanic basalt is pummelled into a granular material over time, forming the ominous-looking jet-black beach.

No tour of the island would be complete without stopping off at one of its many waterfalls. This was my last wish of the trip—to stand under a beautiful, secluded waterfall. Nestled among some giant elephant ear-plants, cascading down a majestic mountain, we found such a spectacle. Because of the light refraction, the water had a mystical blue tinge to it that just begged me to jump in. I did—the falling tons of water damn near broke my neck and knocked my loin cloth right off my behind! I quickly got out of the ice-cold waters.

Before leaving Tahiti we stopped off on the far side of the island for an unhurried lunch. We ate these very appetizing giant shrimp (about 6 inches in length), called "mantis" shrimp, washing them down with Hinano beer (Tahiti's best and only), and sat there a while savoring the cool island breeze. It certainly felt strange not leaving a tip on the table. Around French Polynesia, tipping is considered taboo.

Entry #9   Sept.   ??

I have no idea of what day it is. Being so out of touch with the rest of the world, I seem to have lost all conception of time. It's ironic, but I really miss knowing what's going on in current events; I miss being involved. Isn't this just what I sought to escape by coming here? The only news we receive at the club is strictly by word of mouth. All around the grounds today the words rang out about

Egypt's President Nasser. "Nasser is dead, Nasser is dead"—all day long, "Nasser is dead." I guess Nasser is dead!

There's something else I've come to find disturbing besides the routine fun in the sun, day in and day out, and that is the ever-present odors that fill the air here. The sweet smell of gardenia combined with the overbearing odor of garlic is everywhere around the club. Well, you can't stop the flowers from growing— but the garlic! The goddamn French cuisine is saturated with it. We all reek of garlic breath and there's just no getting around it; being the breath freak that I am, this condition is driving me up a palm tree! Repeated tooth brushing and swallowing pure shots of straight Lavoris out of desperation, were all to no avail. Paradise stinks!

The feature event of the day was the Tamaaraa feast at Bali Hai Hotel. That's where they cook the pig and other delights in the earth–covered oven. I sat down at the table and noticed a coconut with a straw pierced through the top. When I reached for the cool nut milk drink, the straw seemed to be wiggling! I had drunk a Mai Tai or two before dinner, but not enough to create an optical illusion. Sure enough, my eyes did not deceive me; there was actually a tiny lizard clinging to my straw for dear life!

After dinner, we were treated to a "tamure" demonstration by a local dance group. The girls were dressed with not much more than discreetly placed flowers, and by the time their violent undulations had ceased, most of their flowers were shaken off—an unforgetable experience!

Entry #10   Oct. 1   7:00 P.M.
To avoid that horrendous boat ride from Moorea to Papeete, we decided to take the plane again and spend our last night at the Matavai Hotel in Tahiti. This would also avoid us having to wake up at 5:00 A.M. to start the trek home.

Yesterday, at 3:00 A.M., Peter and I found ourselves big game hunting once again. When he was in the bathroom, a 6-inch brown spider crawled onto his foot. It was quite harmless, but the sight of the little monster caused Peter to jump. We christened the creature "Legs Diamond," and promptly knighted him with the sole of Pete's sneaker. Throughout our stay, Peter's sneaker has proved to be invaluable for such services. In fact, we've grown so fond of it that we're going to have it bronzed when we get home!

Entry #11   Oct. 2   4:45 A.M.
Check out the time on this entry, and you'll see why I'm just a

little upset. We haven't had a moment's peace since we turned in for the night. First the wild chickens, and then the damn dogs. They all started whooping it up and they're still going at it! It sounds like an Indian war party out there. If that isn't bad enough, at 1:00 A.M., I got the much dreaded "Tahitian two-step." That's where you get off the toilet, take one step forward, shake your head, no, and take one step back—and there you remain. I have no idea what caused this sudden case of dysentery. We've been drinking the water in Moorea for two weeks with no ill effects; in fact, it was the most deliciously pure water I've ever drunk in my entire life. Peter succumbed to this affliction too. It was funny to see two good friends literally fighting for the toilet. It seemed as though "paradise" was giving us one more kick in the ass! I immediately started to dispense Lomotil, a prescription antispasmatic for such occurrence, and in just two hours, it had settled all fights for the toilet. We affectionately referred to those miracle pills as "binding arbitration"!

Entry #12   Oct. 3   8:00 A.M.
They say that you don't really appreciate your country until you've left its shores. This truism was my happiest discovery of the entire trip. It's nice to go away and it's even nicer to come home.

The other night's ordeal in Tahiti left our strength so depleted that the poor stewardesses had to just about shovel us aboard the plane. From the moment we took off, we encountered tremendous air pockets and everybody was throwing up. Peter and I were just too wrung out to get airsick, so I found myself passing out Dramamine to the less fortunate.

Eight hours later we touched down in L.A., and it certainly felt good to be back on home turf. Although we were like the walking dead from lack of sleep, I coaxed Peter into pushing straight on home without a night's rest. I was intent on reuniting with Janice as fast as possible. Even on the last leg of the trip we weren't spared from torment. It must have been the stewardesses' first flight—they talked loudly, laughed, and threw crackers at one another, and did everything but let us sleep.

The memory of my venture leaves me with two, quite contrasting emotions. After so many years of waiting and conjecture, the realization of the voyage has given me a tremendous sense of fulfillment and elation. Yet at the same time, I'm still saddened by the feeling of utter disappointment. Actually, the explanation is quite simple. The Tahiti as seen through the eyes of Captains Cook and Bligh simply no longer exists. There were no throngs of bare-chested island maidens paddling out to greet visitors; just customs officers very methodically processing us through what seemed like an endless line. Nor were there the large tribes eager to make our acquaintance—merely a select few who were well briefed and choreographed for a staged greeting.

Looking through the travel brochure pictures of the natives, you can't see the mosquitos, V.D., poor skin, and even poorer teeth—all the afflictions which abound there like the palm trees. Tahitians always were and still remain a childlike people who personify a life-style summarized in *National Geographic*: "To sing, to dance, to love, to play the guitar, those are life's aims in Tahiti." Such aspirations contrast sharply with our Western attitudes and temperament. It became abundantly clear that a prolonged stay for an American would be mentally unsatisfying, if not completely boring. Don one hundred loin cloths, intertwine a bushel of gardenias atop your head, and you still can't take one's culture away. There are no havens of refuge from one's self; there are only fleeting diversions.

Come to Tahiti for a vacation, a good time, and you'll never be disappointed. Go there looking for paradise, and all you will find are remnants of a past gone by, strategically placed around the island where it will do the most good. All that I had seen and done there convinced me that "paradise" is something that exists in the mind only. It was time to get on with life in the "real" world; it was time to stop *wasting* time."

As soon as I returned, I was reunited with Janice. She promptly informed me of "her" new dreams in life, which no longer included me! Actually, she gave me an ultimatum: "Quit the force and go into your father's business, or the marriage is off." Well, I'm still a cop so you know how that deal turned out. But I've got to hand it to Janice; the girl knew what she wanted and how to get it.

Unfortunately, I did not apply the wisdom of the Tahiti venture to my other pursuits. Reality had convinced me that there is of course, no garden of Eden. Nevertheless, my quest to find a perfect Eve was unrelenting. But once again, the notion of "perfect," like that of "paradise," is merely a figment of one's imagination; it simply doesn't exist. Believe me, if "perfect" and "paradise" were out there, I would have found them! Instead, I embarked on an odyssey that would last for over a decade. It was a futile search that wound up sounding more like a well-known Christmas carol. Here is the net result of my recklessness: five engagements, four marriages, two divorces, one annulment, (and a partridge in a pear tree!) No doubt about it, if there had been such a thing as "divorce insurance," I would have been in the "assigned risk" category. The only thing that kept me out of debtor's prison was the fact that I never had children and I never had to pay alimony.

I paid a dear price for those past transgressions and not in just a monetary sense. Every last dollar could have been written off as "tuition" for my costly education. But again, I had to come to terms with the idea that my relentless pursuits had cost me ten years of life—more wasted time. Even less excusable was the fact that I had caused a lot of pain in other people's lives. None of those ladies ever misrepresented themselves, never expected me to be anything other than the man they "thought" they had married. Being unwitting participants in my folly, these people's lives were interrupted, their time wasted.

I was looking for a "10" long before anyone had ever heard of Bo Derek. Of course, there's no such thing, so the marriages were destined for doom before they started. If only I could have seen the movie first. In the "better late than never" department, luck and good sense finally prevailed and the fourth time around, I married Bonnie. That marriage is alive and well and our relationship is living testament that reality is its own reward.

If I had to come up with a moral to this chapter, I would put it this way: I, like the alcoholic or drug abuser, wasted a lot of precious time searching for something that does not exist. I, like they, hurt too many innocent people along the way. It's perfectly all right to have fantasy in one's life, so long as it does not govern that life. Dreams should serve the dreamer and not the other way around. Fantasy is okay, so long as no one gets hurt.

SIX

WHEN THE BOUGH BREAKS

For the first time ever, I was completely satisfied with life in the present. I was no longer looking to escape into a past remembrance or a past triumph. I was no longer muttering, "Wait until next year." I was enjoying a new life-style of subdued contentment. Marriage to Bonnie had turned things around 180 degrees for the better. It was as though I'd been given a reprieve, another chance at life in the *real* world, another chance to discover that reality indeed, has its own rewards. At age thirty-five, I was at last growing up. Good riddance to my past! I was living the "right" life with (finally), the right wife. Things couldn't have been better nor could our family have been closer. But this feeling of well-being, was merely the calm before the storm and was destined to be short-lived.

There is nothing mystical about being killed by a drunk driver. Every cop can attest to that. Yet to this day, I cannot explain the bizarre events that shrouded my father's death. The chain actually began when that young drunk killed my father's mother some forty years before. It continued when the ambulance driver ran me down and nearly broke my back. But not even Jimmy the Greek could have foretold the following events.

Sunday, February 5, 1983 was to be the last day I would see my father alive. It was a good day, just like old times, just the two of us. I had invited Dad to go to the Livingston Mall with me to see an exhibition of ultralight aircraft. I had read articles written on Monterey, California, and their new patrol program that used this kind of craft for air surveillance. In a state of wishful thinking I had convinced myself that this kind of program was just what was needed in my town, and I was hell-bent on piloting a similar program (literally). It was just one more of my hair-brained schemes—anything for a thrill. Nonetheless, it was reminiscent of the good old days, when just the two of us would go looking for our next boat for the new year. Only this time, I was asking for his opinions on the subject instead of he soliciting mine. It was a form of role reversal. I wanted to do for him what he so often had done for me. I wanted him to feel included; I wanted him to feel needed; I wanted him to know he was loved.

Our excursion to the mall was a significant piece of irony that preceded my father's death. I often thought it strange that when my dad stepped out of that stunt plane forty years earlier, he would view his mother for the last time. Little did I know that when we left that aircraft exhibition, we'd be seeing each other for the very last time. By some quirk of fate, aviation had become a common denominator in both tragedies.

Things began to get stranger. Later that afternoon, while conversing with Bonnie and me in our living room, Dad suddenly started to joke around about dying. He always maintained a curious if not morbid sense of humor about the matter. I know that he had a real fear about suffering the same agonizing fate that his father succumbed to. He could never have handled such a long-term illness. Often in the past, he'd make me promise that if something like that ever happened to him, I was to "put an end to it fast." He'd make several suggestions on how his instructions were to be carried out, always joking about it, yet always deliberate about what he was saying. It had become the Waimon tradition to make jokes about the things that scared us the most, to never telegraph our fears.

After a few more of his grizzly jokes, he suddenly stood up and made a strange declaration. With both arms outstretched, he looked at Bonnie and me and said, "I'm going to go quick, just like this." Then, with a resounding clap, he brought his hands together. To this day, I often wonder if he had some sort of premonition about his impending fate. The hands smacking together was frightfully similar to two cars striking each other head-on. Whether it was intuition or just an amazing coincidence, I'll never know, but Dad had predicted his own demise with incredible, if not *deadly*, accuracy!

That evening, my father started packing for his business trip up north. Concerned about a predicted snowstorm, he decided to rent a front-wheel-drive Chevy Citation. He figured that it would give him better traction than his own car. But then he asked if he could use mine—a four-wheel-drive A.M.C. Eagle. This was a superior snow car and was also known for "crash survivability." But suddenly he decided against it, concerned about an inconvenience to me. I insisted that he take it, but he declined. I should have *begged* that he take it; it would have spared me a lot of guilt later on. But, Dad, as always, was more concerned about my safety and insisted that I keep the better car. That night, he rented the Chevy; I would never see him alive again.

It was Thursday, February 9, 1983. I was due at the station for the 4:00 to 12:00 shift, but I left for work early that day, allowing myself time to do an errand fo Dad. Before he left, he had asked if I would stop off at his ex-partner's house that day and pick up some memorabilia from his years with Barmark Kitchens. The house coincidentally, was one street away from our Livingston home on Dawson Terrace. After discussing old times, I loaded my car with the boxes of nostalgic articles and drove off. But I didn't drive far. I couldn't resist the opportunity to visit the old neighborhood. I suddenly found myself knocking on doors of some old friends and once in, rehashed highlights of the "good old days." No trip down memory lane would be complete without a visit to the old homestead. The residents there were very gracious and immediately invited me in. After a few moments of getting acquainted, they allowed me to tour the house. The kitchen my father had designed, the built-in bedroom furniture he had constructed two and a half decades before, it was all still there, exactly as I had remembered. As I walked through the house, an avalanche of warm remembrances came tumbling back. It was odd, but for years I had heard and read testimonials of those who had a close brush with death. They all recounted the same bizarre story—the one where they see their whole life flash before their eyes. Well, I was experiencing the same sensation, but ironically, it wasn't me who was about to die.

The 4:00 to 12:00 shift proved to be fairly uneventful. I welcomed the quiet. In the solitude of the squad car, I relived the rush of memories that were rekindled that afternoon. They reinforced the fact that despite the setbacks, life had been pretty good to our family. Before I knew it, 12 A.M. had rolled around—time to go home. Dad was returning home that night and I was anxious to see him. I couldn't wait to see his face when he opened that box of history his partner had given me. It was 12:20 A.M. when the front door bell rang. I had been waiting in the den, expecting to hear the electric garage door raise. This was always the way he came in so I thought it was odd that he'd be using the front door. When I opened it up, I was startled to see two imposing figures standing there. A somber-looking sergeant and an uncomfortable looking patrolman—from the Parsippany Police Department. The look on their faces was all too familiar to me. I had darkened many a doorway with the same look pasted on my mug. I didn't even wait for the word; I just put my arm around Mom and braced her for the inevitable. Strangely enough, at that very moment, I felt sorry for those brother officers. They were obviously wishing they were somewhere else, so I wanted to make it easier for them. I knew exactly what they were feeling and that was—*helpless!* I just said, "My father is dead, right?" The sergeant bowed his head and said: "I'm afraid so." Mom was devastated, but she held her own, once again showing her courage. The details we got were very sketchy. All the sergeant could tell me was that Dad's car had been in an accident and had gone off the road. Since he wasn't able to tell me if another car was involved, I assumed that he had sustained a heart attack and had driven off the highway. Dad had pushed himself so hard and for so long, a coronary would not have suprised me. After I was told where my father was taken, I offered the two officers some coffee. Anxious to be somewhere else, anywhere else, they promptly declined the offer and immediately took their leave.

Mom understood that I had to go to Dad, who was now at Chilton Memorial Hospital, in Pompton Plains, New Jersey. But first, I had to wake Bonnie and tell her of the news. Bonnie totally flipped out, and refused to accept the fact that he was dead. The two had become extremly close ever since our marriage; it broke my heart to see her reaction. Still dressed in my uniform, I threw on my coat and took off, leaving Mom and Bonnie crying on each other's shoulder. Finally, with no one else looking on, I dropped the tough guy act and broke down. For the duration of the ride, I allowed myself the luxury of the tears. But within a matter of minutes, I would learn the hideous truth about my father's death. Then, and ever since, there would be no more tears, only rage, unrelenting rage. I was about to learn what happens, "when tears don't work."

Once in the emergency room, I was greeted by two officers from the West Milford Police Department, Lieutenant James Dykstra and Patrolman Ronald Oblinger. The patrolman had done the accident report and was the first officer at the scene. The lieutenant was called in after the call. He was an expert at accident reconstruction, and by the time I had arrived, Lieutenant Dykstra had sorted out the grim details. In restrospect, I remember quite vividly how the lieutenant treated me that night. He looked like a leftover teenager from the 1950s, right down to his G.I. crew-cut. He was impeccably dressed and had that scrubbed, poster-board look of what a cop is supposed to look like—your basic hero type. In fact, I later discovered that he had received the state's second highest award for bravery when he saved the life of two fishermen who had fallen through the ice. But despite his macho appearance, he spoke in a slow, very gentle voice, which had a calming effect on me. The guy was a real professional.

Off in a corner, the lieutenant dropped the bomb. He informed me that my dad had not died of a heart attack but was killed by a drunk driver! With incredible patience, he reconstructed for me the tragic chain of events.

At approximately 10:30 P.M. that evening, a drunk driver who had been arrested before for driving while intoxicated was traveling on the same rural highway in West Milford that my father was on. Coming in the opposite direction on this two-lane, 40 mph road was a 38-year-old drunk. It was later determined that he had a blood alcohol content of .217; more than double the legal limit. Traveling at a speed estimated in excess of 80 mph., the drunk driver lost control of his car and careered off the road, taking down someone's mailbox. Attempting to recover, the driver overcorrected and sent his vehicle rushing right into the oncoming lane. It immediately sideswiped a car traveling in the opposite direction, splitting open the face of its driver. Dad was just moments behind this driver, but because of the bend in the road, he could not have perceived the impending danger. Once out of the bend, there was no place to escape to. The car was in his path, having ricocheted off the first victim's auto. The drunk driver, with the much heavier vehicle, slammed head-on into my father at a combined speed estimated to be 120 mph. Dad had on his seat belt, but it didn't help. The impact broke the motor mounts and drove the engine right through the dashboard and into my father's chest. His torso was crushed to a thickness of just five inches. As for the drunk? Besides a cut on his head, he was just fine. There were two men who arrived on the scene first. They tried to render assistance but the situation was hopeless. One of the men then summoned the police as well as the rescue team. The car was so badly mangled that it took over an hour for the team to cut Dad free from the wreckage. It was a ghoulish sight.

By the time Lieutenant Dykstra was done relating the story, my eyes were bone dry and riveted on the stairway that led to the upstairs room where my father's killer was now resting. In a blind rage I made a dash for the stairs that would lead to my own form of "curbside justice!" I seemed to be in some kind of trance, hell-bent on avenging my father's death. Pushing open the door, I immediately spotted my enemy, his eyes closed, passed out in a drunken stupor. As if with a will of its own, my hand almost mechanically dropped onto the butt of my magnum. Just as I was about to "clear leather," I felt a firm, yet gentle hand rest on my left shoulder. It was Lieutenant Dykstra. In his uniquely soft-spoken manner, he was able to thwart this reckless intention. He knew that he couldn't physically stop me, but he made it painfully clear that the consequences of my rage would devastate my remaining family even more. His words were compelling—they were literally disarming. The man who killed my father will never know, (unless he reads this book), just how close he came to becoming the second fatality of this tragedy. Both he and I owe a great deal to Lieutenant James Dykstra. He not only kept me from taking a life, but he also prevented me from throwing my own away, no small feat under the circumstances.

Stop and consider these events for a moment. What would you have done given the same set of circumstances? What would you have *wanted* to do? I was suddenly realizing the vast difference between a death and a killing. With the former, there were tears, but with the latter came blind rage and a flood of emotions I'd never experienced before. Not even thirteen years of police work could have prepared me for such an event, nor for what was to follow. Now I was faced with yet another grim detail—identifying my father's body. This was to be the cruelest irony of all. Peering beyond the white curtain at my father's twisted, mangled body, it suddenly occurred to me. I was playing out the same scenario that Dad had played out, forty years earlier. He had come to the hospital, clad in an Air Corps uniform, in 1943 to identify what was left of his mother. Now it was me who had responded in kind, also in a uniform, also to identify the remains of a parent. All those years of wondering what went through his mind that day. I no longer wondered. I finally understood.

Out of consideration for my family, I'll delete the gruesome description of his appearance. I'll just quote the "cause of death" as certified by Passaic County Medical Examiner: "Fractures of the skull, ribs and extremities, with lacerations of the brain, lungs, liver and spleen, with external hemorrhage." In short, everything that could be crushed, broken and ruptured was broken, ruptured and crushed.

After concluding my business in the hospital, Lieutenant Dykstra asked if I would go to West Milford Police Department to retrieve my father's personal effects. I agreed, but asked if he would permit Officer Oblinger to accompany me for the drive up; he agreed. Once in the car, we dropped all the professionalism and simply started to talk to each other. I quickly learned that Ron had seen a lot of action in Vietnam. I knew, because he wasn't talking about it. I peppered him with questions regarding my father's death. "Do you think he suffered or was he killed outright?" Do you think he saw it coming or was he unaware?" These were the morbid questions I had to ask; I simply had to know. Ron, like Lieutenant Dykstra, was patient and compassionate. He realized that no matter how many questions I asked, I was really asking only one: did he suffer? He assured me that my father had died on impact. I accepted his word; it's what I wanted to believe, what I *had* to believe.

After picking up Dad's personal effects, I offered my thanks to the two officers and headed on home. All the way back, I kept on rehearsing just how I would break the news to Gail and Chuck. It wasn't a detail I was looking forward to. Once home, I got out of the car and was about to shut the door when I noticed the two boxes on the back seat. In all the excitement of the day, I had neglected to bring in the stash of memorabilia I had picked up earlier. I scooped up the parcels and headed for the door. This was incredibly ironic. Under one arm I carried the bloodied personal effects worn that day by my father. Under the other I carried over thirty years of my father's past. Why, I asked myself, on this particular day, did Dad send me back to retrieve things from his past? What was the compelling force that made me, on *this* day, go back to the old house to relive my own past? How was he able to predict his own demise with such deadly accuracy? Why did he suffer the exact same fate as his mother did, forty years earlier?

SEVEN

THE TRIBUTE

The following day, Chuck and his family drove down from their home in Connecticut. Desite his initial shock, he was suprisingly well controlled. As a matter of fact, he was behaving in an almost businesslike way; something was very strange. Then I noticed his eyes; they had that thousand-miles-away stare, totally devoid of emotion. It was as though his body was acting entirely independent of his mind, like he was there but he really wasn't. He didn't cry so I knew that his tough, "I'm in control" act was merely that—an act. My brother and I were using the same scheme to forestall the grief. We simply denied it. We allowed only anger to pervade our minds. It was our ploy to exclude all other emotions and drive our overwhelming grief into a state of dormancy. The charade worked, allowing us to function under these trying conditions.

Chuck and I had to make all the funeral arrangements. Mom and Gail were in no condition to assist us in this process. They were still shell-shocked and totally grief-stricken. In other words, they were behaving like normal people! My brother and I decided that we would see to the details ourselves. We decided to go to the Menorah Chapel in Union, New Jersey. It was just over the town line of Millburn, an important consideration. My brother officers had offered to provide a police escort to the cemetery. With the chapel just a stone's throw from headquarters, it was one less thing to worry about. We had also heard that the Menorah Chapel had a fine reputation whose integrity was beyond question. In short, they weren't a rip-off.

Once inside, we were greeted by the owner and escorted to his office. He was a professional as well as a gentleman and at no time did he try to take advantage of our emotional state. In fact, when it came time to pick out a casket, he started out by displaying his least expensive merchandise. He was totally soft sell—none of those high pressure tactics I had anticipated. As it turned out, he didn't have to sell us anything; we sold ourselves. Almost light-heartedly, Chuck and I started to deliberate about a selection. Having been a kitchen designer for almost forty years, Dad had a deep appreciation for beautiful hardwoods. Just a plain pine box was, of course, out of the question. We knew that he was partial to cherry wood so we decided on that. Ironically, we later found out that the last kitchen he designed—for his associate, installed the day before Dad was killed—had cabinets constructed of solid, hand-rubbed cherry. The price tag of the coffin reflected its quality—top cabin all the way. We thought it a befitting gesture. Then, almost jokingly, we discussed the availability of a cement liner to encase this beautiful piece of woodwork. Once again, we recalled Dad's morbid sense of humor when he'd kid us about his own funeral. He also told us not to spend a lot of money. Dad always said that life was for the living and that we should take the money and spend it on ourselves. He told us that we should just dig a hole and dump him in, maintaining that "the worms were going to get me anyway, so what's the difference?" If there were a Jewish version of an Irish wake, that's what he would have preferred, party and all!

Knowing how our father hated bugs, we thought that the cement crypt would protect the beautiful coffin and him from the inevitable infestation. Again, we joked to the director as to this being a parting gesture to the "Old Man." I turned to Chuck and said: "We're burying him in the right wood; we're keeping the bugs out; what more could Dad ask for?" I could tell by the expression on our host's face that he seemed a little puzzled. I'm sure he was used to dealing with people who were a lot more somber-looking than we were!

After we were done, we jumped in the car and headed home. Chuck and I hardly spoke the entire way back. It was as though, for the moment, having taken care of business, we were able to drop the tough guy act. This was the pattern we were setting up for ourselves, outwardly acting be cool, calm, phony. Then when no one was looking, we would drop the false bravado, and enjoy the luxury of just feeling crummy.

As soon as we returned home, the sky opened up; it was about to snow on our parade. The bad weather was turning into a major blizzard. We were growing concerned about hazardous road conditions that might hamper a respectable turnout for the next day's service. But for the moment, there was little we could do about the situation, so we decided it was time to do something for ourselves. Chuck grabbed a bottle of Wild Turkey bourbon and two shot glasses, and off we went to my downstairs apartment. Neither one of us drank bourbon, but there we were, tossing down one shot after another, toasting Dad's memory with each round. It tasted absolutely vile, but after the third shot, I hardly noticed.

Since I seldom drink, I was properly blitzed by this point and inner truths were starting to surface. I never could lie under the influence of booze, so our little session was becoming both introspective and therapeutic. With no one around to impress, we spoke freely about our devastating sorrow. Suddenly, I made the remark to Chuck, "Aren't we becoming the ultimate hypocrites? "A drunk killed our father, and look at us—drunk!" Chuck's reply was swift and bitter, "You're right, we're drunk; but at least we are *not driving!*"

Before I downed my fourth and final drink, I posed yet another question to my younger brother: "Why are we drinking this God-awful stuff; why Wild Turkey?" His reply was that Dad, when he drank, usually drank a mix that was always made with Wild Turkey. It was yet another tribute to our late father. In the face of adversity, we had remained composed and behaved the way Dad would have. We were about to bury him in a casket made of cherry, Dad's favorite wood. Now, we were even drinking (despite its taste) Dad's favorite liquor. We knew that he was gone forever, but identifying with our father's personality, behaving like him, becoming just like him, was perhaps a subconscious unwillingness to let Dad go.

As the afternoon progressed, I was becoming increasingly concerned about how my father would be eulogized; what would be said as a final tribute? I wanted it to be right, I wanted it to be accurate, I wanted it to be perfect. The only way to ensure that, was simply to do it myself. I decided that I would not only write the eulogy but I would read it as well. I felt that I owed it to my father, and was compelled to make this a final gesture. In no way, however, did I intend to upstage the gentleman who would deliver the initial tribute. Though my father was not an overly religious man, Rabbi Samuel Cohen had remained a dear and close friend of the family. My folks were one of the founding families who helped foster the creation of Temple Beth Shalom of Livingston, some thirty years earlier. Dad personally built the pulpits that were originally used by the temple, and designed and donated the kitchen. Our affiliation with both the temple and its rabbi had gone back a long way.

I'll never be accused of being a religious man, but I am notoriously nostalgic. Rabbi Cohen had seen us through other family crises and had shared in our good times as well. Since he was so much a part of our lives, it seemed only appropriate that he'd be the one to officiate the service. It was just another piece of irony that would soon be added to the growing list: Rabbi Cohen had presided at my wedding ceremony nine months earlier. That was the happiest day of my life. Now he would be among us again, this time to share in the worst day.

I awoke early the next morning to bright sunlight; the blizzard had ended and the plows were already mopping things up. Just as I was starting to regard the clear weather as a good omen, the phone rang. The chapel was calling to inform us that because of all the snow, the cemetery workers were unable to open the grave. The memorial would take place as scheduled but the burial would be postponed to a later date. I wasn't that unhappy about this calamity. Actually, I preferred that the trek to the grave site be a private one. I wanted our goodbyes to remain personal; a last gathering of just the family. After the phone call, I put the finishing touches on Dad's eulogy, got dressed and off we went in the big black limo.

We arrived at the chapel early, yet some people had already come. I had hoped for at least a moderate turnout of about one hundred people. In light of the blizzard however, I was concerned that my expectations may have been a bit optimistic. But as the double doors swung open, people came rushing through as though the floodgates had opened up. The sudden onslaught took me by surprise. At first, I thought that all these people had somehow entered the room by mistake—spilled over from another service. But the mistake was on my part, not theirs. Blizzard notwithstanding, within just thirty minutes, over 450 people had jammed into the chapel. The crowd was so huge, the funeral director was forced to open up two extra rooms to accommodate the influx. To deal with the huge crowd, another service that was to occur simultaneously had to be delayed; the mourners were placed on hold in a downstairs room. For those who couldn't fit into our service, the directors rigged a P.A. system to the front of the building so they could hear what was going on.

I was stunned! We just couldn't believe the turnout; it was bewildering. What had my father meant to all those people? Why had they braved such weather and journeyed so far, just to pay a tribute? "Just what kind of man was my father?" These were the questions that surged through my mind. Outside of the funerals for fallen brother officers, I had never witnessed such an attendance. As I immersed myself in the crowd, I ran a gauntlet of well-wishers who provided me with answers to my questions.

The stories I was hearing were heartwarming and remarkably similar: "Do you know that your father helped me start my business?" "Do you realize that your Dad loaned me the downpayment for my house?"—"Helped pay for my kid's education?" The stories of his kindness and benevolence persisted for over an hour. People were literally grabbing me by the arm; everyone seemed to have an interesting anecdote that just had to be told. Just about everyone concluded their story with the same comments: "You know your Dad gave willingly and never said, "Look what I did for you" or "now you owe me." ... "He was a giver, in the true sense of the word, and with no strings attached!"

I was overwhelmed. It wasn't that I didn't believe what I was hearing; it was just difficult to imagine how often I was hearing it. All these stories about one man's generosity and humility; all this for a guy I only knew as "Dad." I think I learned more about my dad in just one hour, than I had in the past thirty-five years!

Just before the service was to get under way, I noticed a large, imposing figure standing in the doorway. To his left, was an attractive, dark-haired lady that I assumed to be his wife. Mom noticed them at the same time and immediately rushed over to greet the couple. Judging by the quickness of her stride, I realized that these people must be very special, so I followed her. After an emotional embrace, my mother formally introduced the couple to me. With her hand firmly clasped around the man's, she said, "Larry, this is Frank and Jo Ann Marinello, they're from Lake George."

This was all I had to hear. I had been so composed up to this point. But this game had run its course and suddenly, my defense shields began to crumble. Hearing "Lake George" had sent me back through time, and a wave of warm memories came rushing over me. Trying to maintain my stage presence, my immediate concern was to hide my tears that were now beginning to form. Under the guise of a hug, I used Jo Ann's shoulder to hide my face and skillfully wiped away the tears and regained my composure. I tried to distract myself by engaging the two in conversation. They informed me that their trip down from the lake started the day before. What was to be an easy, few-hour drive turned out to be a fourteen-hour nightmare. They had driven right into the blizzard and the treacherous conditions had forced them off the road several times. "Why," I asked them; "Why in God's name did you risk your life to come down? Why didn't you just phone or drop us a card; we would have understood." In a voice riddled with both emotion and purpose, Frank recounted a story that was vintage Matt Waimon.

A few years back, Frank and Jo Ann decided to start their own kitchen design service in nearby Saratoga, New York. My father had stopped by to see if the Marinellos wanted to handle the line of cabinets he was representing at the time. For whatever reason, it just didn't work out, so they shook hands and parted company. A few months later, Dad was in the area again and decided to look in on them to see how the business was progressing. In a word, the answer was "slowly." They had a showroom but no display in it, and they needed an acceptable name for their store. The three started talking and within a few minutes, my father was able to resolve at least one of their problems—a befitting name for the business. The name for Barmark Kitchens, my father's company, was derived from a contraction of the names Barbara and Mark, the children of my dad's former partner. Using the same technique, Dad put the first parts of Jo Ann's first and last names together and came up with Jomar Kitchens. Frank and Jo Ann were ecstatic and the name was immediately adopted.

They were so impressed by my dad's accomplishment that they decided on the spot to handle my father's line of cabinets after all. But they still needed a design for their showroom. Once again, and without waiting to be asked, my father volunteered his services. Late that night, and in the dead of winter, Dad asked to be taken to their showroom. Frank informed him that it was 15 degrees below zero outside and that the store front had neither electrical service nor heat. But the intrepid designer would not be deterred. Dad then drove his car around to the front and aimed his headlight directly at the glass-faced showroom. For the next few hours, the two shivered like Jello as all kinds of measurements were taken. "It was so cold," Frank exclaimed, "that the pen your Dad was using actually froze up and refused to write!" They emerged from the igloo at 3:00 A.M. in the morning. The finished product represented over thirty-seven years of award-winning expertise. The happy couple were thrilled with the results and appreciative toward my dad beyond words.

There remained but one problem and that was money. The couple needed a temporary loan to pay for the new construction of the showroom—roughly $20,000. As the company was a newly established business with no real track record, the bank denied the loan. Frank got my father on the phone just as he was ready to leave his hotel for the trip back to New Jersey and told him the disheartening news. "Your father sounded more angry than I was, and told me not to move, that he would be right over." Frank went on to say, "It seemed like I just hung up the phone and there he was! He didn't even bother to come in. He just blew his horn wildly and motioned Jo Ann and me to get in the car. All he asked was, Where is your bank? Without a clue of what he was up to, Matt drove us to the bank that had just turned us down and ordered us out of the car. He stormed into the place as if he owned it and demanded to see the bank president. I guess he knew your dad meant business, so without delay, the president invited us all into his private office. Your father, in a quiet, yet firm voice, demanded to know why our request had been rejected, especially since we owned a house and had the collateral to cover the loan. The president started to stammer and stutter and obviously felt intimidated by your father's line of questioning. Your Dad referred to his unsatisfactory answers as a bunch of gobble-dy-gook, the term my father often used for double talk. Then, Larry, without saying another word, Matt reached into his pocket and pulled out his wallet. Finding what he was looking for, he threw what looked like a document onto the man's desk and said, Here, is this enough collateral to cover the loan? What it was, was the bill of sale to your Dad's new Mercedes, which had less than a thousand miles on it. He was fully prepared to co-sign the loan.

"I don't know if the bank president just wanted to get rid of us or he had actually seen the error of his ways, but by the time we left, I had a check in my pocket, and your dad had a bill of sale still in his; it was quite a performance!"

Frank concluded the story by telling my mom and me what we already knew—Dad did not want to be thanked. "All the way home, Jo Ann and I tried to thank your father for all his generosity, but he just didn't want to hear it; he kept changing the subject. Now do you understand? Now, do you see why we *had* to be here today?"

My question had been answered. But now Frank and Jo Ann had a "why" question of their own. They reemphasized the fact that they and my father had only met on just two occasions. In other words, they were virtual strangers! "So why," they asked, "was your dad so willing to help us; to actually risk so much money on us? Why was this stranger willing to trust us?"

I wasn't really prepared for such a question, let alone a responsive answer. But this time, Mom interceded; she had an answer. She explained to us all that when Dad had the opportunity to buy into his partnership at Barmark he needed a few thousand dollars that he just didn't have. As distasteful as the prospect was, he knew he had no choice but to borrow the money from a friend or family member. First he approached the people whom his father had loaned money to in the past, but they turned deaf ears. In fact, only one person was willing to help and that was my mother's aunt. She wasn't a rich lady but she wanted to help and she believed in my father. The loan was quickly paid back. When our aunt's husband died suddenly, Dad took it upon himself to see that she would be provided for for the rest of her life. It was a commitment he had kept for over thirty years. My aunt, who is now 92 years old, never could find the words to express her gratitude, nor would my father have wanted her to.

Dad never forgot her act of generosity during his time of need. From that time on, he always had a soft spot for people who were just starting out—those who were sincere, hard-working, and honest. My mom told the Marinellos, "Matt saw these qualities in the both of you. He was intuitive in that regard and didn't have to know you long to know you well!"

Frank and Jo Ann had their answers. This time it was they who had the tears in their eyes. This time it was they who reached out to hug us. In a soft, sullen voice that belied his powerful size, Frank vowed to honor my Dad's memory by making a success of their business. I told them both that by justifying my father's confidence in them they would pay the best tribute that could ever be.

To this day Jomar Kitchens (now in Clifton Park, New York) is one of the most successful design services in the area. My Dad's opinion of the Marinellos was well founded, and their continued success is all the acknowledgement my father would have wanted.

Suddenly, it was time for Rabbi Cohen to deliver his eulogy. But by now I had heard so many eulogies by so many people that the event seemed almost anticlimactic. Nevertheless, our dear friend was his usual eloquent self, and the gathering was visibly moved. Fearing this moving account of my father's life, I had desperately tried to block out the rabbi's words. My eyes had to be dry for the upcoming ordeal. But his uncanny ability to knock down walls with words made keeping my composure very difficult. Then came the expected announcement: "And now Larry has a few words he would like to share with you."

Before I started to speak, I studied the expressions on the faces in the huge crowd—expressions of wonderment and concern. I didn't know if I would finish, but the words came and I began.

"You know, my father always maintained a macabre sense of humor about death and his own mortality. He always said, "Wouldn't it be great if I could sit up in my coffin, and see by the turnout just how I was regarded?" Well, let me tell you. If he could only see this enormous gathering, he would have been totally humbled! Your presence alone is the best tribute there could ever be. From the bottom of my heart, thank you all for coming. Now, I ask for your indulgence just one more time, for just one more tribute." I looked at the casket and said, "This is for you, Dad."

EIGHT

NO-MAN'S-LAND

Several days after the burial, we were still receiving baskets of fruit and dozens of flowers. Our house took on the look of a botanical garden! Realizing that the fruit would only go bad, we decided to give the baskets to various police departments in the area. Chuck and I decided that it would be appropriate to make a delivery to the West Milford Police Department. Since they had been so kind to us, we also decided to make a donation to their Policemen's Benevolent Association fund. Mom wrote out a check and off we went. There was also another purpose for this excursion. We still had the grizzly task of sifting through the wreck of the rented car Dad had been driving. Lieutenant Dykstra had informed us that our father's display samples were still in the back of the car. We were escorted to the police impound lot where the wreck was towed to. It was an awful sight. The car was crunched up so badly there was no way of telling what make it was until we found the "Citation" nameplate on the back end. Before we looked in, my brother and I walked around the car at least three times, trying to reconstruct the accident.

Throughout this whole nightmare there remained one nagging question: "Did Dad see it coming?" We all knew that even at age 62 he had incredibly fast reflexes. As a former pilot, he was not the kind to give in to panic. I kept recalling the air crashes he had walked away from and how he always chose to stay with his ship instead of bailing out. He was so cool under fire. If he had seen it coming, he would have taken evasive action, he would have at least turned the wheel! Why didn't he? "Did he see it coming?" The question was still plaguing us. But mercifully, and once again ironically, we were about to have our answer.

From the outside, the mangled wreck was a gruesome sight. But inside, it was downright horrifying! The first thing I noticed was the twisted steering column and wheel, evidence of the tremendous impact. I could see the engine; it had blasted right through the firewall and dashboard. It was hard to believe just how little space remained between the wheel and the backrest of the front seat. I kept picturing my father's body, his chest crushed to the thickness of but a few inches. Then we noticed all the blood; it was everywhere! I wanted to leave, but instead I just sat there on the passenger's side and stared at that damn wheel. I remained there for some time trying to imagine what my father's last moments must have been like. A tap on my shoulder from Chuck brought me out of my trance. We continued to search the car for belongings. Then I noticed something familiar on the floor in the back seat. It was Dad's little pocket tape recorder. He traveled with it on long trips, often dictating memos for his secretary to type out upon his return. We jokingly used to refer to it as the "black box." We were about to realize just how fitting a connotation this really was.

I don't know why, but for some strange reason, I decided to replay the tape. The recorder had a deep crease in it as though it had been struck by something. Perhaps I just wanted to see if it still worked. To this day, my brother recalls the stunned look on my face as the words on the tape were played back. For the first two minutes, we heard our father's familiar dictation, instructing his secretary to compose a letter to one of his clients. Then came a pause at the end of a sentence. A fraction of a second later, we heard what sounded like an explosion. We weren't sure what it was so I backed it up and played it again. This time we heard not only the same sounds, but what sounded like echos to the original blast, which were then followed a minute later by the sound of strange voices.

My head suddenly snapped up with the realization of what we were hearing. I immediately looked over to my brother whose expression confirmed the discovery. Dad, by some quirk of fate, had unwittingly recorded his own death! It was all there—the crash, the car continuing off the road striking the trees, the people who stopped to try and help. We heard them ask: "Are you all right, are you all right?" We heard one say to the other, "Get me a blanket and then call the fire department." The tape lasted only fifteen minutes, but it got it all; just like the flight recorder on a major airline, just like the "black box!"

We could hardly believe our ears; it was like some cruel hoax. First he had predicted his own demise, and now he had actually recorded it! I asked Chuck; "What in God's name is going on

February 9, 1983. The fatal wreck. (*Photos, Cindy Terhune*)

here?" He was dumbfounded, and just sat there shaking his head; there could be no logical explanation to all this.

There was a long and eerie silence throughout most of the ride home. Then just before we arrived home, I remarked: "Dad was a real trend setter. Who else have you known would have recorded his own death?" His only response was: "At least now we know the answer; he didn't see it coming and now we have the proof!" Chuck was right. The question that would have plagued us for the rest of our lives was now answered, and ironically, by my father himself. The tape had proved that he had not perceived the danger. There were no final remarks, nor any screams of terror. There was simply an end to a sentence followed by an end to a life. From time to time I play that tape. Some people think it's morbid but it brings me peace of mind. Sometimes, I just like hearing his voice.

When we returned, I showed the "black box" to my mother. Before I could say a thing, Mom blurted out: "Where did you find that? Your father always kept it in his chest pocket!" Then I remembered Dad kept it there so he could dictate and drive at the same time and still have both hands on the wheel. That explained the blood and the deep crease on the recorder; the dent was evidently the mark of the steering wheel. I then casually hid the recorder in my back pocket, fearing that Mom would detect this new evidence of the impact. Mom refused to hear the replay; listening to his voice again would only have hurt. But she did take comfort in knowing that her husband had not perceived his impending doom. Nothing more was said, so I went downstairs and carefully hid the recorder in the back of my drawer.

With no more well-wishers hanging around, we were finally alone. Sleep up to this point had been intermittent at best, so I looked forward to a much-needed rest. But for the next three nights, my sleep was punctuated by the same recurring nightmare. The dreams centered around that night at the hospital. In it I'd be asked to once again identify the twisted, bloodied remains of my father. The dreams were incredibly vivid and hard to shake off. After being tormented for three nights straight, I decided that I'd had enough.

I quickly discovered that the best way to avoid the nightmare was simply not to sleep. So I allowed myself to be mesmerized by the T.V. For hours on end I'd stare aimlessly at the tube until I simply passed out (which was usually after the fourth channel played the "National Anthem".)

For the next several months, the television became my haven of retreat; my escape from reality. I had become insomniac, often averaging only two hours of sleep a night. At least I had the good sense to realize that I posed a danger to society once I put on my uniform. I quickly asked to be removed from patrol duty in order to avoid a poor judgment call once out on the road. There was no question that driving a police car and my ability to shoot straight were greatly impaired by my lack of sleep. But there was a more serious threat to be considered. I had built up a great deal of hostility and seemed to be mad at the world. I was angry at the judicial system that had failed to protect my father from this previous offender. I was a part of this system, so I suddenly resented my own job. I now had a huge grievance against all drunk drivers and was afraid that I would release my savage fury against the first driver who so much as smelled like booze!

With my "black belt" came a great deal of discipline and restraint. As long as I've worn a uniform, I never once hurt anybody out of malice. But now there loomed a bonafide prejudice towards intoxicated drivers, and my ability to control myself was now in doubt. Sergeant Barber, who was sensitive to my state of mind, placed me on desk duty.

My life-style had become relatively simple. I could be found either behind the desk at headquarters or in front of the tube at home. I quickly convinced myself that every drunk driver in America was out to get the Waimon family. Considering our past encounters with drunk drivers, I felt that my paranoia was well-founded. Going out on the weekends was simply out of the question. That's when most of the drunks traveled and I wasn't about to tempt fate again. Before long, I put restrictions on all the nights in the week except for my normal work days. Using every excuse in the book, whether real or imaginary, I quickly severed all ties with the outside world and reality itself; now I felt safe.

My self-imposed exile from life went on for months; the challenge to "live again" went unanswered. Never before had I allowed life to intimidate me like this. Because a drunk had lost control of *his* life, I was now losing control of *mine*; it hardly seemed fair. Nevertheless, I was unprepared to fight a problem that I couldn't even admit I had. Here was a classic case of "denial," the ever-present companion of the drug abuser and alcoholic. How can you begin to deal with a problem if you're unwilling to admit that one exists? To illustrate my state of mind, I honestly believed that I had no problem.

WHEN TEARS DON'T WORK

Our small downstairs apartment had become my sanctuary. Bonnie, trying to keep her sense of humor, rechristened it the "Bat Cave"—an appropriate name considering that I kept the room in total darkness. The only light source there emanated from the T.V., which was fast becoming the nucleus of my existence. I was watching so many "Honeymooners" and "Star Trek" reruns, that I was actually able to lip sync with the scripts! With the room always dark, I often lost track of what time of day it was. Sometimes my only reminder was when Bonnie would sarcastically yell down, "Larry, it's time for dinner, would you like to "beam up?"

Bonnie was becoming increasingly alarmed over my behavior. She tried to get me to talk about my anger and the hurt. I just sat there and made my trite little jokes. Then she took drastic action and hid the T.V. remote control, which angered me. Frustrated and in tears, she shouted out, "You act like I just sabotaged the Star Ship Enterprise!" An apology would have been an admission of guilt, and I was too far gone to admit to anything. But I knew that I had hurt her and I didn't like that at all. To make it up to her, I stopped cruising the galaxies with Captain Kirk, and for a whole month I gave up my beloved "Star Trek."

Now, banished from the decks of my "star ship," I had to find a new world to live in. Relocation was as simple as changing channels. With one press of my command module, I had gone from the cosmos to a more earthly place—Pine Valley, the home of ABC's soap opera "All My Children." If it wasn't for the fact that the L.A. Raiders are ardent fans of this soap, I wouldn't have the guts to admit that I'm a loyal viewer. In fact, you'd be astonished to learn just how many cops I know watch this show religiously! They're just afraid to come out of the closet. It isn't considered macho.

Nevertheless, I quickly got hooked on this show. It was yet another form of escape, another way to live vicariously through the actions and exploits of others. My mood on any given day was soon determined by the show's scriptwriters. If my friends in Pine Valley were happy that day, I too was happy. If one of the characters was being abused or victimized, I also felt violated. When things got really bad, they would put a call out to "Pine Valley's Finest," Detective Young and Lieutenant Borelli. These two guys were the worst bunglers I had ever seen! They were so bad that if they tried their damndest, the two couldn't even catch a cold!

Whenever they appeared on the screen, I'd literally shout insults at them; as policemen they totally offended me.

As with most soaps, the show was punctuated with its share of miserable characters, those who constantly stole, lied, cheated and brutalized the others whom I'd come to regard as "family." The only bright note in the entire show was the unwavering love between two of the central characters, Greg and Jenny Nelson. But because the girl who played Jenny decided to leave the show, the writers decided to eliminate the character by killing her off. Well, I—and a few million other fans—were totally outraged! She possessed some of the only redeeming qualities to be found in all of Pine Valley.

By then, I was slipping in and out of reality so often that the difference between my two worlds were indistinguishable. Psychiatrists refer to what I was doing as "projecting." By projecting myself into a world other than my own, I was able to avoid dealing with my personal hurts. In other worlds, I appeared almost stoical over the loss of my father; no tears, no emotion. Grief was the reality I had subconsciously denied. But once in Pine Valley, all emotional restrictions were lifted. I could laugh, shout at the tube, and (if no one was looking) I could even shed a tear or two.

Sigmund Freud would have had a field day with me. Over the loss of a father whom I had loved and revered for thirty-five years, there was no crying, virtually no expression. But kill off a favorite T.V. character, and the complexion of things changed dramatically. I became animated, I became enraged; there were tears! All this emotion over a fictional character who never existed! Be that as it may, I wasn't about to take this loss lying down. Frustrated by a story line that had become depressing, I decided to phone the American Broadcast Company and voice my displeasure. I was determined to save Pine Valley from total damnation!

The switchboard operator must have detected the urgency in my voice and within a minute, I was actually speaking to a publicist for the network. Her name was Audrey Fecht, a very kind and gracious lady who allowed me to ramble on at great length. I compared today's soaps to those aired in the 1950s. I explained that other than a cosmetic difference, the story lines have remained virtually unchanged. But back in the fifties, they performed a necessary service. Adultery, divorce, and other such skulduggery provided necessary escape for bored housewives leading sedate, mundane lives. But in today's world, divorce and the like are commonplace; things I see every time I go on patrol. I told Ms. Fecht that if I wanted to view the kind of unhappiness I'd been seeing on "All My Children," then I might as well remain at work and collect overtime! I insisted that there was enough misery in everybody's life without having to be constantly reminded about it. The need for escape is just as real as it was back in the fifties. I merely suggested that the brand of escape be altered to reflect people's preferences. Then I asked Audrey to consider the long-running success of "Love Boat." It was nothing more than a floating soap box. The huge viewing audience illustrated a genuine need for the "happy ending." It never mattered how entangled things became during the hour-long show. Everybody knew that by the end of the cruise, Captain Steubing would have righted all wrongs.

I urged Ms. Fecht to consider the market potential of the happy ending notion. "At least," I pleaded, "put some balance back into the show." When Jenny was alive there was some wholesomeness to the program. Deep-sixing her, robbed the town of its "balance" and the viewers I spoke to felt cheated! All that seemed to remain in Pine Valley were a bunch of contemptible individuals. There was no one left to stand up and cheer for. Half jokingly, I suggested that they rename the show: "Murphy's Law," since whatever can go wrong in Pine Valley does go wrong. Then I made my closing pitch. Trying to convince Audrey that I represented the show's typical audience, I suggested that it was in the network's best interest to submit to the will of its viewers. "If the episodes didn't start to lighten up", I told her, I and probably a few million other loyalists, will simply turn off the T.V.!"

Audrey Fecht is the kind of person who would make an excellent hostage negotiator. The lady sure knew how to handle a crazy person! When I phoned, though I sounded very cool and deliberate, I was really in a highly agitated state. By the end of our conversation, Ms. Fecht had assured me that my comments did not fall on deaf ears. In fact, a significant alteration of the story line would be soon in coming. Of course, when the next nice thing occured in Pine Valley, I went boasting to other fans that it was all my doing! Taking it one step further, I actually lectured to my fellow viewers on the subject of "apathy." "Let this be a lesson to you," I'd say, "don't just wait around for life to pass you by; go out and make things happen!"

At this point, a big net should have been dropped on my head; I was obviously out of my mind! Imagine my having the audacity to lecture on life passing one by? After forfeiting a year of my own to the tube, I was in line for the "Hypocrite of the Year" award! In fact, had it not been for life on T.V., I would have had no life at all. I was existing in no-man's land, addicted to television much the same as an alcoholic is to his booze. Though reckless T.V. watching poses little threat to society, psychologically, I was no better off than your average drug abuser. I was hiding from my problems when I should have been out trying to solve them. My inability to cope with life in the real world had propelled me into an empty, unproductive existence. Though I had accused my father's killer of leading the same life-style, my patterns were becoming similar to the very man I hated! But the comparison had gone unnoticed. I would have denied such a notion anyway.

Finally, something snapped. I attended my first group meeting of Mothers Against Drunk Drivers (MADD of Morris County, New Jersey.) This particular chapter was founded by Donna and Pat Ferrante, in memory of their daughter Dawn, who was brutally killed by a drunk driver on Thanksgiving 1982. Our family had previously presented Donna's chapter with a check for $5,000. The money had been raised by colleagues of my father who belonged to the American Institute of Kitchen Dealers and who later founded the Matt Waimon Memorial Fund.

Prior to the meeting, I spoke to several other people whose families had also been victimized by drunk drivers. I listened to one horrible story after another; each story sounded remarkably similar to the one before it. Some people spoke to me of their enormous grief and others detailed their frustrations. But the common denominator to each and every story was the bitterness in the voices. There were no tears, no quaking speech. There was just anger and plenty of contempt for both the drunk driver and the judicial system that had failed to protect loved ones. Suddenly it hit me! I saw in these people's faces exactly what I had become—cold, bitter, silent, unable to talk about the ordeal except in the company of other victims.

The guest speaker that evening was a clinical psychiatrist who specialized in the treatment of posttraumatic depression. The first thing he did was to differentiate between natural and unnatural causes of death: "Heart attack, brain tumor, kidney failure; these, as tragic as they are, remain natural causes of death. Family and friends get to mourn the passing through natural or conventional means. Tears, discussing the loss with loved ones, we make our tributes and then we go on. By contrast, death by auto, vehicular homicide, manslaughter, no matter what name you give it, it still adds up to the same thing: It's *not natural*. Therefore, the family of the drunk driving victim does not respond in a natural or conventional way. The avenues of response that are normally available are often denied to the family of such a victim. These people often don't show tears, and in too many cases, they're unable to or unwilling to vent their enormous rage and bitterness. They become obsessed with getting even with the person who caused all this grief, and start dwelling on a befitting form of vengeance! But soon these people realize that there can be no justice, at least not the kind that they are seeking. Overwhelmed with unventable anguish, the survivors of the victims now become the victimized ... As you might have guessed already, when I refer to these people, I'm really referring to *you* people, but unlike your deceased loved ones, your suffering is an every day affair. In every sense of the word, you are all victims!"

I knew that he had hit the nail on the head. I said before that you can't begin to resolve a problem until you can admit that one exists. Once we realized that we were all "victims," it was somehow easier to acknowledge our personal torment. "Victims have a right to speak out," the doctor, "so let's talk about it."

One by one these people stood up to speak. First, there were only words of anger and bitterness—all the things I had heard before our guest spoke. But after the initial venting, some of the more personal and deep-seated feelings began to surface. People talked about the guilt they were experiencing over their loss— that it should have been them that got killed instead. Many people blamed themselves for what happened. "If only I had insisted that my husband [or my daughter or my son] not go out that evening." But most of the participants concluded their remarks by saying, "I feel so helpless because I couldn't do a damn thing to prevent what happened."

As if he expected to hear this, the doctor responded, "Do not turn the knife on yourself. "None of you are to blame, nor could you have prevented what happened. There is only one person to blame here, and that's the drunk driver. If you can accept this fact, the healing process can begin to take place. If however, you allow your grief to be overshadowed by your anger and unwarranted guilt, this thing is going to beat you."

One of the more honest members asked the doctor, "How do you know if you've been beat already?" He answered, after commending her for having the courage to ask the question, "You're in deep trouble when you constantly "project" yourself into other dimensions. If you often fantasize being somewhere or some-body else... This would indicate an unwillingness to accept what has happened. In your fantasy land you can simply avoid all those pains that are just too overwhelming to deal with. It's a very simple case of denial. How many of you watch a lot of daytime soap operas?" I immediately slid down in my chair. I was start-ing to feel a bit uneasy, as if the doctor had singled me out in order to make his point. Mercifully, I was saved from embarrassment when strangely enough, just about everybody raised their hand! Almost immediately, discussions broke out among the mem-bers. The room was alive with chatter; everybody was compar-ing notes from their favorite episodes of various T.V. soaps. I concluded that I wasn't the only one who was living in Pine Valley.

Once again, the group had mirrored my own sorrowful state of affairs. But it was impossible to refute the logic of the doctor's point; a show of hands had confirmed it. We were all using var-ious ploys to hide from our agonies. Losing ourselves to the tube was only one method. Now, however, I was able to realize that my abnormal behavior was indeed quite normal. I was just as screwed up as everybody else. I now felt a great deal of kinship to everyone in the room. There was no more embarrassment, no more pretense. Now I had the courage to participate in the dia-logue. I told the doctor how my life had become so completely intertwined with a daytime drama. I even admitted my attempt to alter the show's script. The revelation didn't seem to surprise him; in fact, he used it to dramatize his final remarks.

"All of you have sustained an incredible loss. All have lost a loved one. To various degrees, you have also lost some of the control you once had in your life. But as you all now realize, the destinies of both you and your families are often in the hands or control of others. Larry, like most of you, is feeling a little in-secure these days and more than a bit vulnerable. His desire to control a show's script underscores a desperate need to regain control over his own life. Unfortunately, things are not that sim-ple. Control is often an illusion, dictated by the whim and reck-lessness of others."

The doctor had been painfully accurate and frank. At the very least, he had identified the symptoms that plagued far too many innocent victims. A symptom can't be treated correctly until the cause has been properly diagnosed. I knew that it was now time to take up residence in some place other than Pine Valley; it was time to move on. But the move would be postponed a day or two. A far greater challenge was now imminent—one that would require all the inner strength I could muster. In just two days, I would be facing down my father's killer in a court of law.

NINE

VICTIM'S DAY

The moment I've been waiting for is fast approaching. Fifteen months of daily obsession and sleepless nights. Over 450 days of planning, scheming, and wondering, all to the exclusion of everything and everybody. Just 24 hours to go; one more day, and I'd be eyeball to eyeball with my father's killer. The posturing by both sides is over, an agreement has been reached, the plea bargain accepted. Justice is out of the question, but there must be punishment; I must realize my pound of flesh. I've been assured my day in court but will the judge allow me to speak? If he allows me to speak, will he listen? If the judge listens, will he also hear? I must be heard. After all this time and heartache, I must be heard. After all this time and heartache, I must have the opportunity to avenge my father's death . . . "

What you've just read was taken directly from a diary I kept throughout our ordeal. Entries were made when I needed an outlet but couldn't afford the shrink's ninety-dollar an hour fee. Doing so provided only marginal relief, but it helped stop me from punching walls. The following is excerpted from the same diary, recorded while the thoughts and emotions were still fresh in my mind.

"Of course there was to be no trial: the plea bargain took care of that notion. The early morning court session was to include a sentencing hearing and the actual sentence (if any) of my father's killer. Naturally, in anticipation of what lay ahead, a good night's sleep was out of the question. For once, I was grateful that I had to work midnight to eight the night before the case. Patrol work distracted me, yet afforded me time to review my speech. As the hours passed, I rehearsed what I was going to say to the judge, (if given the opportunity), and how I was going to say it for maximum effect. When I was satisfied with the speech, I rehearsed it all again. All that I wanted to say and accomplish for the past fifteen months was pumped into this effort. I knew that at best, I'd get only one crack at this. It had to be perfect; I had to reach him; I had to make it work. Time was encroaching on me and I was weary. But suddenly, happily, the rehearsals no longer sounded rehearsed; I was ready!

Finally, the sun had come up but I was growing increasingly restless. The anticipation was overwhelming and once in headquarters, I started to pace like a caged animal. The sergeant, who was sensitive to my plight, allowed me to leave early. I bolted out the door and quickly made my way home to pick up Mom before heading off to court.

The ride down was a tense one, to say the least, and the strain was beginning to show. A few jokes, some nervous laughter, and suddenly we were there. Before we went in, I reassured my mother that everything was under control. I told her that somehow Dad was with us this day, that it was his day—Victim's Day—and that we weren't about to be slighted.

Once inside the courthouse, we immediately caught the attention of some of the court deputies. In all my haste, I had forgotten that I was still wearing my uniform. Camaraderie among police has always been high and it was apparent that this upcoming case, since it involved a brother officer, was attracting a lot of attention. Soon we were besieged by a bunch of blue-shirted well-wishers who offered both comfort and support to my mom and I. It was a display of consideration and kindness that I had not expected. With all this attention, I hardly noticed the man in the wheelchair who had entered the building. Then it occurred to me that he was the defense attorney in our case. I remembered being told that he enjoyed a fine reputation but was now afflicted with a degenerative disease that impairs speech and cripples the body. As I watched him struggle down the hallway, I couldn't help but ponder his bleak future and his personal courage. I wondered if this man's condition would in any way influence the outcome of the case; would sympathy cloud the real issue? Then suddenly, there he was, my quarry, the man who killed my father. Our little forum quickly grew silent, sensing some kind of confrontation. It wasn't hard for him to spot our imposing looking group; we were occupying the entire width of the corridor! What was most intimidating, however, was not our sheer presence, but the obvious silence! I never knew that silence could be so loud. I could hear distinctly the cadence of his feet as it reverberated off the granite floor. I could hear my own heartbeat. At that point, I released my mother's trembling hand and advanced to the front of the pack. My uniform was conspicuously different from those of the deputies and the contrast set me apart from the rest of the group. Almost immediately, the man who killed my dad concluded who I was; contact was finally made. His stride stopped dead cold, but it was his eyes that told the story. They bulged, then darted wildly about. He was scared and obviously would have preferred a more congenial route to the courtroom. Nonetheless, he had no option but to run the gauntlet of solid blue, and I was enjoying the dilemma. For the first time in fifteen months I wasn't feeling like a victim. Now it was I who was the predator and I was taunting my prey with divine relish! As he continued to walk, I indulged myself with one final gesture. When he was just a few feet from me, I was able to glare directly into his eyes. When assured of his attention, I began to toy menacingly with the butt end of my pistol. He paled at this gesture; my point had been made. Certainly many of the onlookers caught that action. One of the deputies laughingly reminded me that what I had just done was nothing short of intimidation. I quickly retorted: "No, it wasn't; it was just a demonstration in body language!"

After thanking my brother officers for their support, it was time for us to head for the courtroom. As we made our way down the hall, we were intercepted by the assistant prosecutor who had been handling our case. She was a very kind and concerned person but she was about to throw us a real curve. For reasons I'll never understand, she explained that she had been substituted in this case by yet another assistant prosecutor. Changing horses in midstream was most disheartening and made no sense at all. I tried to put aside our frustration and hastily reviewed the case with this new quarterback. It was immediately apparent that this individual was ill prepared to prosecute the State's case. I then turned to my mother and told her that we were in big trouble. Aware of our new predicament, out of patience and out of time, I asked him to grant me but one request. I wanted the opportunity to address the court, and I literally begged him to see that I got it.

At last, the stage was set and we all took our seats. Joining our little entourage was Mrs. Rodriguez from the victims-witness support program. Throughout this whole experience, her ever present support and compassion had been significant and much appreciated. Just on the other side of the aisle sat the defendant; totally emotionless, skillfully avoiding my stares. As Judge Vincent Hull got the first case underway, the hardest part was about to begin—the inevitable wait. As this was only a sentencing hearing and not a trial, I had hoped that our case would be heard first. As the hours passed, my mother, who throughout this ordeal had remained a pillar of strength, was now starting to show the signs of stress. Sharing the courtroom with her husband's killer had grown increasingly intolerable. Meanwhile, I continued to observe the cases and how well these matters were being adjudicated. Happily, I concluded that Judge Hull was not only consistent and fair but he was also very tough, a real "hanging" judge. I was encouraged that I might indeed get an opportunity to speak. I began to stir with nervous anticipation. One more glance at my mother's face and I realized that we both had reached our limit; it was time to act. There was a momentary pause in the action, so I seized the chance to confer with the prosecutor. I don't know if it was the urgency or just the tone of my voice, but nonetheless, we got results. Almost before I could get to my seat, I heard the judge announce our case. After a short preamble of opening statement and motions, Judge Hull uttered the words I had prayed for: "I understand that the son of Matthew Waimon would like to make a statement. Officer Waimon, you may approach the bench." Taking a couple of quick deep breaths, I rolled my eyes towards the ceiling and muttered, "This is for you, Dad."

Once again, I became acutely aware of the silence; it was nervewracking. By the time I passed the defendant and the two news reporters, my breathing had become rapid and shallow and I was rubber-legged. Could I have come all this way only to be beaten by myself? I finally began to speak.

The following is taken from the court transcript.

"First of all, Your Honor, on behalf of my family and all of those concerned about the drunk driving issue, I wish to thank you for this opportunity. I'm a little nervous, Judge, so please forgive me if I stammer or suddenly get "gridlock" of the mouth. I realize that what I'm about to say is a bit long-winded. But bear in mind that by condescending to this plea bargain I have already saved the state a lot of time, not to mention money, so please indulge me.

VICTIM'S DAY

"Your Honor, we didn't come here to seek justice. As with all death by auto cases, there is *no* justice! Now if this sounds a bit bizarre, then consider this: If I were to steal a man's car, I'd probably spend more time in jail than if I were to drive drunk and kill the man in it! There are states in this country that actually provide a stiffer sentence for those who kill deer out of season! Your Honor, there is something very vulgar about a law that places more emphsis on animals and things than it does on human life!

"Judge Hull, you and I know that death by auto is only a fourth degree offense.* Punishment for such a heinous crime hovers on about the same plateau as that of a repeat shoplifter. How can I expect justice from a system that does not differentiate between a theft of clothing and the theft of a human life?

"To try and seek justice in this matter would indeed be an exercise in futility. But I did come here for a reason, Your Honor, as well as for a purpose. The reason I'm here is simple. I would like to diffuse some of the bitterness and contempt that I feel towards the system that you and I are very much a part of.

"We perpetrate a fraud on the public, Judge Hull. We give people the illusion that we can protect them from the wrath of the drunk driver; we can't. We make them believe that there is a punishment to fit this brutal crime; there isn't! My ability to protect an unsuspecting public and your efforts to punish these offenders have been thwarted by those with the *real* power to reduce the carnage on our highways. Those at the very top of the judicial system, the lawmakers, they're the ones with the most power and they're the ones who have accomplished the very least. Their complacency and indifference towards senseless human suffering absolutely astounds me! I just don't understand their apathy towards the victims of drunk drivers. I can't understand why they don't create laws that would protect the public and deter drunk driving. I'll *never* understand why death by auto only merits a fourth degree punishment!

"Your Honor, if I were to get drunk, pull my service revolver and haphazardly fire into a crowd, there's little doubt that I would be charged with murder. But if I were to drive drunk, hurl a two-ton weapon into the crowd and kill a child, there's no doubt in my mind that I would get away with murder! This isn't justice Your Honor, it's just plain lunacy.

"Judge, for the past fifteen years, I've borne witness to an inept system that fails to protect the public. I've stood in their doorways; I've seen their looks of terror and utter disbelief. I know

113

what it is like to feel totally helpless, unable to console, unable to quell their anger and their ultimate despair. It is a detail that no cop relishes; it's an experience one never forgets. In all my years of police work, it was hard to imagine one that is worse.

"Your Honor, on February 9 of last year, I realized what worse *really* was. It was when fellow officers came to *my* door with that familiar, helpless look. It was when they told me that *my* father was dead. It was when I knew that I would never see my dad again. That's what worse *really* is. As in similar cases, the shoe can't pinch till it's on your *own* foot. It's the only appropriate adage that comes to mind. Unfortunately, your Honor, it takes a personal tragedy such as this to convince a person that drunk driving really *is* a crime.

"Judge, as you may already know, this was not our family's first experience with a drunk driver. Forty years ago my father's mother was brutally killed by a drunk driver. The convertible she was driving was struck broadside when a young drunk ran a red light. She was decapitated and mangled beyond recognition.

"For years, Judge Hull, I could only imagine what it must have been like for my Dad. At the time, he was only 23 years old. He was an Army Air Corps instructor and was performing aerobatics when the tower radioed up with the tragic news. I can't imagine how he was able to land the plane safely. A war was on, his father was dying of cancer, and now he had to identify his mother's mutilated body. I could only wonder what it must have been like for my dad because he never spoke or complained about his early torments.

"Your Honor, the day my father was killed was the very day I stopped wondering and I stopped imagining. The man who killed my Dad ended my years of conjecture. I no longer guess, I know exactly what my father had gone through. I have experienced the same horror, the same grief, the same frustration and rage that he had felt a generation ago. I too, have been left with reccurring nightmares and indelible memories of that fateful night. I too, have to share a courtroom with the man who killed a family member and since the laws are as antiquated as they were forty years before, I shall realize no real form of justice.

"What happened to our family was nothing short of highway robbery. We were ripped off, cheated, pure and simple, and we're damn mad! But don't make the same mistake I did, Your Honor. Don't assume that our grief and anger are limited just to our family. The day of my father's funeral quickly vanquished that thought.

"Judge, the day of the service was preceded by the worst blizzard in ten years. Nonetheless, even with the inclement weather, people managed to show up. They trekked in from as far away as California. They came from all over; 450 people arrived and soon there was just no more room and people had to be turned away until room could be made. I milled around the room, Your Honor, totally flabbergasted, wondering what all those people were doing there. I hardly recognized anybody and was starting to think that some dignitary had died and that they were all in the wrong room! Out of the corner of my eye, I then noticed the funeral director pointing towards me and my family. Suddenly, everyone lined up and proceeded over to offer condolences. What seemed like an endless line continued on at great length and much to the chagrin of the director, who was obviously concerned about another service that was due to begin. But everybody had a personal story that just had to be told, and these anecdotes continued on for over an hour.

"I heard from one family how my dad had made it possible for them to start their business. Another couple explained that had it not been for my father's assistance, their daughter could never had gone to college. But the story I cherished the most, came from one of my dad's former employees. He recounted a story I vaguely remember, though my father never talked about it. It was about a co-worker who had been hired by my dad and his partner under the most unusual of circumstances. The man had recently been released from prison after serving time for embezzlement at a bank. The conditions for his parole were that he had to get a job, and that he must reside in the area. Whereever this man went, the door was always shut in his face. With a wife and two children to support, the situation was getting desperate. The former employee then told me that not only did your father hire the gentleman, but they put him in charge of looking after the funds; they treated him as an equal. This man justified my father's confidence in him by becoming an honest and diligent worker.

"Judge Hull, these stories of one man's kindness and benevolence towards his fellow man were overwhelming. I think I learned more about my dad in one hour, than I had in the last decade! I had not been aware of his accomplishments and deeds, simply because it wasn't in his nature to go around tooting his

115

own horn. He never told anyone he helped, "Look what I've done for you" or "Now you owe me." He never wanted homage for any of his generosities, and thank-you's always embarrassed him. Dad simply enjoyed helping people; he was always a quiet giver.

"By his own peers, Your Honor, my father was acknowledged as one of the best in his industry. He started out with nothing and with no one's help, but with a lot of courage and perseverance, he earned his success, but he never forgot his humble beginnings. His biggest pleasure came from the sharing of his talents and energies with those who were just starting out. Others who had come to rely upon my father's expertise, tenacity and prowess in the industry, have already suffered appreciable economic setbacks. Those who had depended on his friendship, his wisdom and strengths for so many years, they too, now have to endure without him.

"I realize, your Honor, that all of this sounds like some sort of eulogy, but my father's modesty would have forbidden such a tribute. The things I mentioned about his life and his deeds were simply observations made by others. I related the story merely to emphasize my original point, that all of us, family, business associates and friends, have *all* been victimized by this savage crime. Make no mistake about it, Your Honor, this is one of the most brutal crimes around. One of the survivors of the three-car wreck is here in this courtroom; she'll verify that assertion. She almost died that night and now endures untold suffering that includes brain damage and paralysis. She too, would like to know why drunk driving is not regarded as a real crime. She too, wonders why the system allowed the defendant to drive, soon after a prior drunk driving arrest. She too asks at whom should she vent her rage; at the man who couldn't control his drinking or at the system that wouldn't control the man? Sitting next to that victim is yet *another* victim, Your Honor, and that woman is my mother. I won't even attempt to tell you how she feels; I couldn't do an adequate job. To lose both your spouse *and* your best friend all in one day is hard for me to comprehend. This coming summer, my brother, sister and I, were all planning a very special party for a very special couple. For over two years we've been putting together a surprise party for my parent's fortieth wedding anniversary. Well, Judge, we sure got the surprise; but thanks to a certain drunk driver, there sure as hell isn't going to be any party!

"Your Honor, you have graciously allowed me to ramble on for the past several minutes. But for the most part, I have related the plight of others whose lives have been affected by this tragedy. But I would like to conclude this dissertation on a very personal note and specifically tell the court how *I* have been affected by this crime.

"I never needed to hear the accolades of others to realize what a great man my father was. The fact that he was a great Dad was all I ever cared about anyway. How ironic it is that a great man such as he could have been killed by an individual whose only claim to fame is that he drives drunk a lot, killed a man, and hurt a lot of people.

"Your Honor, the day of my father's funeral service, I was the one who delivered the eulogy. When I was done, I noticed that the only dry eye in the house was that of my own! People quickly remarked how brave I was and how well I was holding up. I didn't cry then, nor have I ever since. I never cried, but *not* because I'm brave, and *certainly not* because I'm holding up well. I don't cry because I have found the magic elixir for tears; it's known as rage, and it occupies my mind and my heart to the exclusion of all other emotions. The man who killed my father, Judge Hull, has denied me the luxury of tears, and now all that remains is bitterness and contempt.

"People often ask me if I ever have nightmares about this tragedy. Well, I used to, Your Honor, how could I not have? My father's death certificate was a nightmare in itself! It read, "cause of death: fractured skull, lacerated brain, ruptured spleen and liver, punctured lungs, broken extremities"; and this was only a *partial* list! In fact, everything my father could have broken, crushed or ruptured *was* broken, crushed and ruptured. it took an hour and a half to cut my Dad free of the wreckage. His chest had been compressed to a thickness of half it's original size. The 80 mph impact had sent the car engine crashing through the dash and into his body. What it was like to hug his crushed and twisted body for the last time is something that even *I* can't describe! Nightmares of that evening's events were something that just couldn't be reconciled. Of course, Your Honor, the best way not to dream is simply not to sleep. To this day, I force myself to stay up just as late as possible. I sit in front of the T.V. until 4:00 or 5:00 A.M. and then I simply pass out. I'm like a zombie for the rest of the day, but it's the only ploy that seems to protect me from the horror show dreams. I even have feelings of guilt over my father's death. The night he was killed, I was on duty, supposedly ensuring the well-being of others; perfect strangers. What it comes down to, Your

Honor, is simply this: Even with all my powers and skills, I couldn't do a damn thing to protect my own father from being killed. Never in all my years of police work have I ever felt more inadequate or more helpless than I did that very night; the whole thing is damn *frustrating!*

"These days, Your Honor, I don't go out very much; I sort of sit home and hide. I seldom socialize and I absolutely refuse to go out with my wife on a weekend night. That's when most of the predators, the drunk drivers, come out on the road. Call it paranoia, but I'm starting to detect a definite trend regarding the fate of my family members. The police psychiatrist informed me that my reaction is normal for people victimized by such violent crimes. It's a form of agoraphobia, the fear of leaving the security of one's home. Judge, if this is true, then I have become my police department's "resident agoraphobic". When I go on duty, I never leave the confines of the front desk. Once I used to be a very active, involved policeman. I used to be a good cop, not a super cop mind you, but a good one nonetheless. Now I'm a "nothing" cop; I just sit there and answer the phone. For the first time in fifteen years of street duties, I have been scared right off the road. For the first time in my career, I am vulnerable to emotions that prevent me from doing an effective job. I can no longer maintain that sense of detachment that is such a vital part of law enforcement. Today, if I were to be dispatched to handle still another drunk driving related fatality, one or two things might happen: I might become overwhelmed by the sight of yet another mangled victim and fall apart, or I might simply grab the drunk driver and rip him apart! Of course, neither reaction would serve in the public's best interest. In light of my present state of emotions, Judge Hull, my career has suffered dramatically and future promotions are, of course, out of the question.

"The only relief I can get from my personal torment is literally not to be found on this earth! Soon after my father was killed, I took up the hobby of flying. I suppose that it was a form of vicarious living, a way of keeping my father's memory alive by reliving *his* earlier and happier moments. Once in the air, I would become totally emancipated from the rage and grief I had left on the ground. But to paraphrase that famous line of Joe Lewis, I can run, but I cannot hide! An appropriate statement when you consider the fact that the first thing I fly over when I take off and the last thing I see when I come down, is the very hospital my dad was taken to the night he was killed. Your Honor, for the surviv-

A son flies in memory of his father. 1984.

ors of 25,000 victims of drunk drivers each year, there simply is no escape from the grief and the anger. This translates into a hell of a lot of human suffering. How ironic it is, however, that forty years ago, it took a drunk driver to knock a Waimon out of the sky. Forty years later, it took a drunk driver to put a Waimon back in the sky! Thus our family tragedy, or curse, has now gone full circle.

"Your Honor, I told you that I had come here for a reason, and that was to vent some of my bitterness and rage. Because of your kindness and infinite patience, you have given me the chance to do so. You may recall that I also came here for a purpose, and that is to ensure that the man who killed my dad never gets the chance to inflict such misery on other victims and their families. I also mentioned that in death by auto cases there can be no justice. My thoughts have not changed, Your Honor, but this in no way means that there can't be some form of *punishment*! There must be punishment, but one that can guarantee the lives and welfare of others. The defendant has displayed a propensity to drink and drive drunk. He had his chances but he chose not to heed the warnings, and now a man is dead. The *only* way you can guarantee that this individual doesn't drive drunk and kill again is to lock him up just as *quickly* as possible, for as *long* as possible. I realize that under the terms of the plea bargain, "as long as possible," may only result in just a few months of incarceration. No matter what fate awaits the defendant, he'll still get the chance that he never gave my father, and that is to go on living his life!

"Never once, Your Honor, has this man ever come forward with his condolences. Never has he ever phoned or written to say that he was sorry for having killed my dad. This man has shown absolutely no remorse over what he has done to our family. Perhaps if he were to have *his* life interrupted, and *his* freedom taken away, then perhaps too, he may develop a new regard and reverence for human life.

"Therefore, Your Honor, I *implore* you to hand down the maximum sentence that the law will allow. Do so, Judge Hull, and you will be helping to right an injustice that has spanned forty years. Do less, Your Honor, and you'll only be adding more insult to our injury.

"Judge Hull, on behalf of my family and from the bottom of my heart, I wish to thank you for both your time and your consideration.

As soon as I turned to walk back to my seat, I felt that I had been purged of a tremendous burden. All that rage and grief I'd been harboring for over a year, finally had been vented. In this regard, I had accomplished what I had come there for. Regardless of the verdict, I was satisfied that I had done *all* that was legally possible to avenge my father's death.

If their expressions were an indication, the people in the courtroom had already determined the defendant's fate. It looked like a unanimous "thumbs down!" Everybody was showing some sort of emotion—grief, bewilderment, even anger. Kind-hearted Mrs. Rodriguez, who was there to render support and comfort to my Mom, was now being comforted and supported by my Mom, as she openly wept. "Okay," I thought, as I took my seat, "I convinced everybody else, but what about the judge?"

Finally, after some paper rustling, and a long motionless stare directed at the defendant, Judge Hull finally spoke. At first I was concerned; he started out by complimenting my speech and the effort and love that had gone into it. He was displaying such kindness and understanding that I was starting to think that he was preparing me for a big letdown. Then he turned his attention towards the defendant and suddenly, his whole demeanor changed. For the next several minutes, he lambasted the drunk driver; I was encouraged. Then it came, the much-waited-for judgment. As the defendant stood up, Judge Vincent Hull passed sentence. The defendant stood there emotionless as the judge imposed the full six-month jail sentence. It was to be served not in the prison annex that he had hoped for, and not on a work release program that his attorney had sought. This was to be straight time in one of the toughest prisons around. In addition, he also imposed a $2,000 fine, a $5,000 penalty to be paid to the Violent Crimes Compensation Board, a five-year revocation of his license, and finally, mandatory involvement with an alcoholic treatment center. He concluded by saying to me that he wished that he could have imposed a stiffer sentence but under the confines of the plea bargain, his hands were tied. Under the circumstances, I was satisfied that the judge had done all that he possibly could have on our behalf. As my father's killer was escorted out the side door by a couple of deputies, shackled in cuffs, I shot my fist up in total jubilation! As I stood up and blurted out to Judge Hull my heartfelt thanks, I turned to embrace my mother. I held her for a long time and then with a quaking voice, I whispered in her ear: "Ma, it's over; it's *finally* over."

121

June 1, 1984

Dear Judge Hull:

On May 24th, you imposed sentence on the drunk driver who
killed my father. The way you adjudicated this matter,
certainly merits comment... Acting as my family's emissary,
you graciously allowed me to address your court. Thus,
fifteen months of amassed anger, frustration and bitterness,
finally was able to be vented. The therapeutic value we
have realized from that privilege, has already proved far-
reaching. Though our grief will always be with us, at
least some of that bitterness and rage, that has plagued
us throughout this ordeal, has now subsided....

I watched you as I spoke that day; I know that you heard
me. But what's more important, I know that you were
listening! You exuded compassion and wisdom, reflected
by your subsequent comments and by the sentence you
imposed.

The word has already gone forth as to what transpired in
your courtroom. Victims of the drunk driver and their
families, have been greatly encouraged by both the sentence, and moreover, by your attitude towards this insidious
crime...

All of us who have felt the wrath of the drunk driver,
appreciate and applaud your efforts. Unfortunately,
complacency and indifference, still pervades the judicial
system. It's the lawmakers who foster the notion that it
is no real crime to drive drunk and kill. The punishment
mandated for such atrocities, bares that out.

I realize that you are only one person. But in this instance,
you are one person who has made the difference! I fervently
hope that other magistrates and lawmakers will soon acquire
your courage and profound sense of responsibility for their
fellow man. When that day comes, then the tide of brutal
maimings and killings, will finally start to ebb...

Most Reverently,

Ptl. Larry A. Waimon

LAW:dlp

Once outside the courtroom, I encountered the attorneys and reporters that had overheard the case. Several of them jokingly offered me jobs at their firm, based on the speech I made and the results I got. Even the assistant prosecutor who sat there motionless throughout the proceedings had something to say. He told me that he had helped me the most, by not trying to help me at all, that I had won it all on my own. While I was slapping myself on the back, I noticed a very somber-looking defense attorney sitting there conspicuously in his wheelchair, motioning me to come over. When I reached by his side, he extended his right hand and offered his condolences over the loss of my dad. Suddenly, my triumph turned melancholy. I knelt down on both knees so that I could look him in the eyes and I grabbed the hand I was shaking with both of mine. I assured him that there was no hard feelings and that I realized that he was just doing his job and that I admired his effort. As I turned and walked away, I again pondered this man's inevitable fate, his fortitude and most of all, his courage. I then thought about my Dad. I remembered his handicaps, his fortitude, and of course, his fate. Then I thought about the man who struck him at over eighty miles an hour, who walked away with hardly a scratch. Why, I thought, does God seem to protect the drunks?

Later that day, we celebrated our so-called victory, by going out for dinner. We joked about a certain drunk driver and wondered how he was enjoying his new life in prison. Then suddenly, our laughter and joking stopped; we all were thinking the same thing at exactly the same time. Dad was still dead, but in a few months his killer would be free to go on living. Indeed, we had won a small battle, but most assuredly, we *all* had lost a war.

We acknowledged our gratitude to both ladies who had helped us through our ordeal, the original assistant prosecutor, and of course, Mrs. Rodriguez. We sent them each a bouquet of flowers. But I especially wanted to thank Judge Hull for his effort and concern. My letter to him is reproduced, exactly as I sent it to him, on page 122.

There is a tragic footnote to this chapter. Early on, I wrote that my squad leader, Sergeant Dave Barber, had allowed me to leave headquarters early so that I could go home before heading off to the courthouse. Though he had been compassionate toward our family, he never imagined that a similar tragedy could ever befall his. But on August 17, 1985, his niece and nephew, his sister's only children, were struck head-on by an unlicensed, 18-year-old drunk driver. Kara Ann McIlroy was only 19, her brother Kurt 21. They were both honor students attending the University of Alaska, Fairbanks. They had their whole lives ahead of them. They both died as a result of their injuries. Their deaths are a terrible loss and have devastated the McIlroy family. I wish to dedicate this chapter to the memory of Kara and Kurt; I grieve for their family.

---

*Shortly after this case, death by auto (vehicular homicide) was upgraded to a third degree offense from a fourth degree offense.

TEN

DENIAL

"Emotional breakdown" is a term that conjures up all kinds of preconceived notions. Screaming, violence and padded cells are the first things that come to mind for most of us. This is to the delight of the movie moguls who capitalize on this, the "darker side" of mental illness. In reality, the overt gestures of the disturbed person usually occur *after* a breakdown has taken place. The violent displays we witness as policemen are merely the symptoms of a more serious and underlying problem. Nevertheless, once the cop has stabilized the situation, he simply leaves, though not much has been resolved.

I seldom pass up the opportunity to ask the shell-shocked family of the victim: "What happened?" It astounds me how frequently I get the same old reply: "I don't know; he, (or she), just went beserk!" All too often, outward signs of emotional instability are not always apparent. In fact, sometimes, swings in personalities are so subtle, so imperceptible, that victims and their families seldom recognize the warning signs. The bottom line is that it is the cause and not the symptoms that is the real culprit here. Left unattended, emotional wounds that are allowed to persist and fester, that are "denied," will eventually lead to some sort of breakdown.

Because we live in a world in which many situations are stressful, *anybody* is a candidate for an emotional breakdown. Yet not all stress is bad; in fact, some kinds of stress are considered beneficial. Just ask the successful executive or the accomplished athlete; they will probably tell you that they actually *thrive* on competitive stress. But for most of us mortals, stress is something we would prefer to minimize.

Policemen, at least outwardly, must maintain a posture of toughness and a resilience to stress. But it is our own fault that we are frequently viewed as "hard guys," often devoid of human emotion. Admittedly, some cops, usually the rookies, enjoy the myth, the demonstrations of "macho." They need to prove to themselves and to their fellow officers that they can handle it, that nothing can unnerve them, no matter how gruesome, no matter how frightening. But for the seasoned officer, the tough facade is merely a ploy, a trick we use to hide our fears, our sadness. To get the job done, we have to be *professionals*. But because we appear cool calm and collected, we are regarded as "cold" and "indifferent."

Nothing could be further from the truth. Some of the most sensitive people, the most caring people I know, are fellow officers. We fight like crazy with one another—sibling rivalry exists in any close-knit organization. But when a brother officer calls for help, everyone comes running. Our problems occur because we try to live up to the myth off duty as well. Cops are notorious for not sharing their problems, even around loved ones. They do what their instincts on the job tell them, and that is to "protect." You protect your family from all the job's horrors. You protect them from the stories of despair. You protect them from your personal pains. We are enslaved by the idea of what a cop should be and we behave like one everywhere. Tragically, there is a very real person behind the uniform who finds himself with no adequate way to "vent" his emotions or his problems.

Without the conventional ways to unwind, police often turn to the unconventional. They start sharing their problems with another person, usually of the opposite sex. This person becomes the cop's confidant and, in many cases, a lover. If that doesn't soothe, they do what many other people do—they turn to booze or drugs, or both. Some even choose the way out that is literally right at hand—the gun. The ultimate escape seems never out of reach. For years, the police profession has had one of the highest rates of divorce, alcoholism, and suicide of any group. These facts prove that cops don't handle their stress well at all; they simply are able to mask it better than others. This isn't dealing with the problem—it's another form of "denial." Because we are afraid to lean, unable to vent, unwilling to show weakness, we continue to wind up lonely, drunk, dead—or all three.

With a tally of three failed marriages, I had certainly had experience with one of these states. But now, hell-bent on self-destruction, I was zeroing in on the last two. It was like trying to win the triple crown of "Worst Police Scenarios!" The only problem I was having was in trying to become an alcoholic on two Bloody Mary's a week. I wouldn't drink before one of my drunk driving lectures, afraid of being seen as a hypocrite. So I limited my boozing to my days off. If I was going to try and kill myself on two drinks a week, I realized that the cause of death would never be cirrhosis of the liver!

As the weeks passed, I grew even more detached from family, friends, the job—everything. The nightmares of my father were starting again, but now I had to contend with new dreams. These were not about his mangled, twisted body; I was used to those. These dreams were worse. They were about the happy times, the best of times—the times we were all together. In the dreams I was able to hug my dad, to hear him, to tell him how much I loved him. We were together again, we were a family again. Then—the reality, the waking to inevitable realization that it was all a dream. The dreams kept on occurring, and I felt tormented and frustrated by the constant visions. Elation—then despair; it went on for weeks.

Throughout this ordeal, I never once confided in Bonnie. I dealt with it the way too many cops deal with their problems—silently and alone. In other words, I didn't deal with it at all! I was hiding from the truth, masking it behind false bravado and morbid jokes. I had lost all sense of reality, and the last one to notice that I had was me.

Bonnie decided that it was time to react. She called the police psychiatrist, Dr. Feldman, and scheduled three sessions in a row. Then she told me that I was going to go, whether I wanted to or not! Of course I protested—the old denial syndrome—insisting that I could handle things on my own. But her order was not negotiable, and the next day off I went to the "head shop."

The dialogue between me and the doctor was incredibly painful and revealing—so much so that I was tempted to omit it from this book, or at least certain passages that were just too personal. But that would be another way of hiding the truth. I decided on a unique approach to help me over this hurdle. I taped all three sessions with the doctor. Listening to them later, I "detached" myself from Larry the "patient" and was somehow able to become Larry the "writer." I simply transcribed everything from tape onto paper, as if I was writing about someone else. I read it back and when I was done, I read it all again. After reviewing it for the third time, it suddenly occurred to me that I was for the first time, finally, hearing the truth. It was hard to accept. For several minutes I just sat there, stunned, totally bewildered. I didn't even notice that Bonnie had come into the room. Seeing my expression, she said jokingly, "You look like you've just seen a ghost!" I didn't answer; I didn't know how to. I had seen something much more frightening than a ghost, I had seen myself; I had seen what I had become, how far I had slipped. This time I was forced to acknowledge the damage, the complete and unrefutable devastation. This time, not even "denial" could protect me. This time, there would be no place to hide. Pull up a couch; "Therapy" is now in session.

ELEVEN

THE SESSION

DOCTOR: Larry, how can I help you?

L.W.: Well, Doc, obviously I've got a problem, but it's not like any kind I've had in the past.

DOCTOR: How so?

L.W.: Well, Doc, this one transcends all my usual neuroses and it's got me stumped. First of all, for once, this is not a bad marriage; Bonnie and I are very happy. As a matter of fact, we're going on four years, which is a new record for me! I haven't even screwed around on her, which as you know, is also a first for me! I suppose that the prospect of AIDS and Herpes keep a lot of us in line! Just kidding, Doc. Actually, I've never been happier as far as a relationship goes. She really is a good friend and you know how important it is to *like* the person you love.

Unfortunately, Doc, this problem I have now is a lot more serious than any other I've come to you with and I just can't seem to shake it. That's also why I booked three sessions in a row, so that this discussion can have some continuity; I really feel the need.

Since my father was killed, I have become very withdrawn, very reclusive. I feel like Howard Hughes, without the billions, of course! You have known me long enough to know how I display sadness and disappointment. I usually laugh about it or make jokes about it. I suppose that I'm too much of a coward to cry, at least openly, so I've always made light of my situation and that's how I deal with my worst problems. But now it's gotten to the point where

I know that I've got a *real* problem and I can't laugh my way out of it.

I'm becoming agoraphobic. I seldom leave my house unless it's absolutely necessary. I'm becoming a "couch potato," watching T.V. hours on end, and when I have to go out, I feel this tremendous anxiety, especially when I have to go to work and deal with people. Not that I ever cared for crowds, Doc, but it's never prevented me from leaving my house. It's kind of a vague anxiety, but it's real and quite debilitating. I'll tell you, Doc, leaving my house is becoming a major event! In fact, I feel so traumatized by even the thought of leaving, that I often call in sick for work, just to avoid having to deal with the people. [At this point, I paused for a long time.]

DOCTOR: Larry, please go on; this is very interesting.

L.W.: Well, Doc; besides the obvious problem, I've got another problem. I'm doing these lectures all over the state on drunk driving. It's kind of ironic that not only does this necessitate me leaving the house, but I've also got to be around a lot of people! It's really funny, almost paradoxical. On one hand, crowds and strange places give me the "wim-wams," and yet I keep putting myself back into the very same environment! In fact, Doc, for every lecture I do, I seem to get three more requests, and I'll tell you, it's really getting to me. The night before a lecture is a total write-off as far as sleep goes. I just lie there staring at the ceiling and holding my twisted guts. I take a Lomotil for the spastic colon and usually a Dramamine for the nausea. I love when people tell me the next day how impressive my lecture was and how *composed* I looked! Isn't that a kicker, Doc? I'm telling these kids how to face the world without booze and pills, and look what I have to go through just to deliver the message. I feel like the ultimate hypocrite!

I'm going to tell you why I came here and it's not for the obvious reason that I'm really screwed up. I came here, Doc, to hear myself admit the truth. I'll lie to myself but I've never lied to you. Maybe I feel if I'm paying you to listen to my nonsense, then I should be entitled to at least speak the truth! Besides, Doc, you've always been a master at extracting the truth out of me with your questions.

About this problem; I know what it is and, most likely what caused it. The trouble is, I don't know how to handle it. Doc—I'm at the point where I'm simply not living any more. It's gotten so bad that I look for excuses, any excuse, to get out of not going someplace, and when I do, it requires tremendous preparation to get psyched up for it, and it's my hypothesis that this whole thing can be attributed to my father's death. I'll tell you why I feel this way. One day I was watching the "Phil Donahue Show," and they were discussing the loss of a loved one and the many ways we cope, or don't, with that loss. One of the guests then went on to describe the loss of his father and how it affected him. It was weird, because when he described his father's traits, it bore a remarkable resemblance to those of my father's. He possessed a type "A" personality—strong-willed, an over-achiever, indomitable, a human success story. The son went on to tell just how much he adored his father and how at the same time he felt intimidated by his father's achievements in life. But then he went on to make a very profound and compelling remark. He stated that it is human nature to look for the "approval" of your father, even after he is gone! So then I started thinking; maybe this is what I am now looking for, this "approval" thing. Remember, I told you about that book I was writing as a tribute to my father? Well, perhaps this is my way of getting a posthumous approval from my dad. I swear, Doc, this book has become an obsession to me. I think about it day and night, almost to the exclusion of everything and everybody else. I also realize that the chances of getting published are pretty remote at best. I suppose that's why I keep doing all those lectures, in spite of all my anxieties. I'm getting a lot of publicity from all this, and the T.V. spots and news clippings are giving my effort credibility. Apparently, my will to succeed is triumphing over my nervous stomach. You know, Doc, it's very strange. All my life I've been a self-indulgent individual who simply walked out or away from a tough challenge. College got too tough? No problem, I'd just quit. Marriage got too rough? No arguments, I would get a divorce. I always took the course of least resistance and up until my father's death, I felt content enough. Now I've got the determination of a pit bull! It's amazing! It's almost as if his will and tenacity was now engendered in me. I know it sound stupid, Doc, but I feel that if my project craps out, that I'll be letting my dad down, or at least, his memory.

DOCTOR: Larry, let me interrupt you for a moment. Do you think that your father would have expected such a tribute?

L.W.: Are you kidding? He would have shunned such a tribute. Like always, it's an obsession that's totally selfish on my part. Nevertheless, Doc, it's a tribute I'm determined to pay. No matter what it takes, I've got to see it through.

DOCTOR: Larry, do you feel that your father wanted you to be in any other profession?

L.W.: If you mean was he sorry that I didn't take over his business, the answer is, no. He always told me that as long as I was doing something that I enjoyed and it was honest, he was happy for me.

DOCTOR: Wasn't he also proud of you?

L.W.: I would like to think so. He used to crack me up. Wherever he went, no matter what town or what county, the first thing he would do was to approach the cop in the street and strike up a conversation. Then, as always, he would whip out his wallet and proceed to show the poor guy pictures of his son, the "policeman!" Like they really gave a damn. It's really funny, Doc, but all my life, it was my dad, the top kitchen designer; now it's ... or at least it was, "My son, the Cop!" [I paused for a long time.] Pardon me for reminiscing, Doc.

DOCTOR: Not at all. Larry, it's very important that you remember these anecdotes.

132

THE SESSION

L.W.: Thanks for indulging me, Doc. You know, he used to wait up for me until I got off the 4:00 to 12:00 shift. It never mattered how tired he was or how long he worked that day, he'd be up. He just loved hearing those everloving police stories. Even when his eyes slipped to half mast, he still wanted to hear it all. Doc, he was always my *greatest* fan. That's when I lost it, Doc.

DOCTOR: What's that, Larry; what did you lose?

L.W.: My enthusiasm!

DOCTOR: For your job?

L.W.: For everything, and especially the job. I told you he was my fan and, yes, he was proud of me. I guess, it was like having that "approval" I spoke about. He was my greatest audience and my greatest reason for wanting to perform. Now the job has become something I hoped it would never be—just a job.

I'll tell you something else, Doc, I've been living in a fool's paradise. I thought *I* was the protector, that I was the tough guy, just because I'm capable of handling everybody else's problems, or because I've got a black belt or a strong body or whatever. But you know what? I'm a phony! I'm like a Hollywood storefront. I look substantial and real from the outside, but step through the door and all one sees is open framework! The real man was *Matt* Waimon, not Larry. He didn't just act tough or capable, he *was*! Because he faced responsibilities and challenges, and I ran from them. Because he was out there taking care of business and busting his hump, I was allowed to live in some sort of fantasy world, guaranteed that Big Daddy would always be there to underwrite all of my mistakes. Funny, isn't it, Doc?

DOCTOR: What's that, Larry?

L.W.: I always thought that as he got older, I was protecting him, well at least from physical harm and God help the guy who tried to hurt him! But now I see that all along it was *he* who protected the protector! I swear Doc, I feel absolutely dwarfed by that man's power even now that he's gone.

Now that I think about it, one of my neighbors came out with a very profound truism. She said that "you don't stop being a kid, until one of your parents die." I think, Doc, this is where my problem lies. For thirty-five years I was allowed to exist as a kid. Even though I felt independent, there was always that ever-present umbilical cord. I'll tell you something else; I think he liked it that way. I suppose if I were a father, I too would want my children to always need me, at least a little. Remember how much my Dad loved boats? Well, he was thrilled over the fact that I could never afford my own. Don't forget, he paid more in taxes each year than I could earn in three! This meant that I always had to be on *his* boat. It also meant that Bonnie and I would vacation with my folks every year in Lake George. This didn't mean that we were indebted just because we didn't have the bucks. It just meant that I couldn't water-ski unless he drove the boat and he couldn't ski unless I drove. He respected our privacy; we really did enjoy each other's company. I know some people thought it was odd that a thirtyfive-year-old would still want to vacation with "Daddy and Mommy," but I didn't care; we all just got along so well; it was great! I'll tell you, Doc, in his last years we really did become good friends and I couldn't get over how close he and Bonnie had become. I'm thrilled that they got to know each other; it was really a shame, Doc, that a lot of kids never have the kind of relationship we had. I never took it for granted. If kids only realized what a luxury it is to have parents around long enough to enjoy them! If only they knew . . . This whole thing just pisses me off.

DOCTOR: What, Larry; the fact that your father died?

L.W.: *No,* Doc, not that he died. I'll tell you just what I've told thousands of people all around the state. He didn't die, he was *killed,* and that makes all the difference. I'm angry. I'm bitter. I want to stop being so miserable, I want to stop hating.

DOCTOR: Who, Larry, who do you hate?

L.W.: It's not so much as who, it's more a case of what; what do I hate? I really don't hate the guy who killed him anymore. But I'll tell you, I used to fantasize about killing him . . . often! Very often. No, Doc, I hate the fact that he got ripped off and by a nobody. I hate that he'll never get to see his grandchildren or enjoy his retirement. I hate the fact that I couldn't protect him.

DOCTOR: What do you mean by "protect him?"

L.W.: I don't know, Doc. I guess what I meant was that because I'm in the business of protecting people, I should have been able to protect him. The day I was protecting the town of Millburn, my Dad was getting killed in West Milford. I know it sounds ludicrous but I feel that I let him down. I hate being powerless; I've always been able to fight back and I couldn't even lift a finger to help him. I don't just feel victimized; I feel violated and I hate the feeling! Maybe that's why I'm scared all the time—afraid to leave the house, afraid of losing control. Maybe this is why I feel so vulnerable. I can't help thinking about it; I always thought of my Dad as indestructible. Then in a blink of an eye, poof! Now you see him, now you don't. I think of "control" as an illusion, determined and dictated by other people's whims. Think about it, Doc. My Dad's mom was killed because a young drunk lost control of his car. I was seriously injured by a drunk ambulance driver because he lost control of his vehicle. My father gets murdered because some bum lost control of his life and his car. God damn it, Doc for three generations our family's fate has been dictated and controlled by those who had lost their control.

You know, Doc, I've never lived in fear. I was always a risk taker, a thrill seeker, an adventurer. Maybe that's why I found scuba diving and flying so exciting. I loved testing my skills and doing things as if my life depended on it—literally! It was a high—having total control, mastering environments I had no business being in. As long as I had control of the activity, my life was my own, I was in charge. Now I realize that I'm *not* capable of controlling my environment and I can't protect myself or my family. I'm so damn paranoid and frightened that I beg my family not to drive at night and especially not on the weekends. I feel that death by auto is becoming the family legacy—the fate that awaits all of us Waimons like some sort of curse! Living in chronic fear, Doc, isn't exactly my idea of living at all. Whatever I'm doing these days, it hardly resembles living. Doc, I feel as though I've seen better days and that it's never going to be as good again.

DOCTOR: Larry, what are you trying to say?

L.W.: I guess, I'm trying to say, why bother? Why should I bother hanging around anymore? I'm not living anyway; I'm just existing; I'm just plain fed up; nothing does it for me anymore.

DOCTOR: Larry, are you saying that you have suicidal tendencies?

L.W.: All right Doc, I'll level with you. But let me say something first. Suicide is something I've always detested. It hurts too many innocent people, and it's an act of a coward, pure and simple. It's everything I've always been against; it's shameful. So now that I have prefaced my answer with all the correct sentiments, I'll still have to plead guilty to your question. Yes, Doc, I do have a preoccupation with suicide. I fantasize about it all the time now. My wife and family have picked up on my little jokes, my little innuendoes about quitting the scene. Maybe I was trying to sample their reactions, testing them to see how capably they'd deal with such an event. Or maybe I was doing just what my father had done so often when he joked about his mortality. Maybe I was preparing them. This is the real reason I suppose, that I'm here today, Doc, and at the insistence of Bonnie. She's really worried, and I guess that my mood changes weren't as subtle as I thought they were. I've been scaring the hell out of her and she literally begged me to make this appointment.

DOCTOR: Larry, let me interrupt you for a moment. This fantasy, as you put it, is a catharsis that—

L.W.: Doc, what is a catharsis?

DOCTOR: A catharsis is nothing more than a purging of one's emotions, often in a way that is morbid. Your reaction to your father's death is a typical reaction, especially when it involves a feeling of guilt. Larry, at this point, I think it's important that I get this across to you. Would you agree that you are obsessed with your father's death?

L.W.: Oh, there's no question about it! Everything I do, you know . . . I didn't have to be a success before he died. I didn't have to write a book. I tried before and dropped it—so what! But now, it's an obsession. Now, if I don't get it going, I've failed or I have failed to pay the proper tribute to him, failed to immortalize him. This is my monument to him. I need to say that he didn't die for nothing . . . all these kids that read this book, maybe, just maybe, one life will be saved and then it wouldn't have all been a waste. He would have wanted something good to come out of all this. I just cannot let him down! Doc, do you know what I'm trying to say? Am I saying it? What *am* I trying to say?

DOCTOR: All right. The obsession with your father's death leads, of course, to this guilt and the question: Is there something that you feel you could have done to save his life? Now, think back, was there something that—

L.W.: Well, the day he was killed, he had asked to borrow my car because it was snowing and my car had four-wheel drive. I told him to take it. But then he changed his mind and said no, that he would simply rent a front-wheel drive car down at Avis. Well, it was a light piece of crap, and his car, known for crash survivability, remained home in the garage.

DOCTOR: You wanted to loan him your heavier, safer car.

L.W.: Yeah, but believe me, you saw the pictures of the wreck, it wouldn't have made any difference. If he had survived only to remain a cripple, he would have begged me to shoot him; you knew the way he was.

DOCTOR: Are you saying that now, to erase guilt feelings, that you didn't press him to take your car?

L.W.: No, no not at all. I'll tell you what the guilt is, and I mentioned it before. The guilt is, while I was protecting one town, my Dad was getting killed in another town, and the guilt lies in the fact, that I couldn't help him; I simply couldn't help him. I mean there's nothing I could have done anyway. I'm realistic enough to know that. But we've always been around to help each other and this one time, I just wasn't around!

DOCTOR: This could be a source of great guilt, couldn't it, Larry?

L.W.: Even though I don't admit to that? Even though I don't realize that?

DOCTOR: Well, it's obviously a very serious tragedy that took place, and you weren't around to stop it, at least this is what's going around in your mind.

L.W.: Yes, you feel helpless. Again, it's that need to have control; I just didn't have control.

DOCTOR: You couldn't control, so that guilt leads to anger, the anger turns on yourself. Subconsciously, this may be why you are having suicidal thoughts. Not because of all the things you had said previously.

L.W.: Well, this may be true; but let me reemphasize my original thoughts. We have always been a very, very tight family. We have always been together. There was a need to protect him like I just said, and I couldn't be there for him. Maybe, Doc, and this thought *just* occurred as I'm speaking to you, I have a need to be with him right now, to have companionship or give protection.

DOCTOR: Is that why you think of dying?

L.W.: Well, that's why I do, I . . . I do. I need to be together again. He was always there for me, and now I've got to be there for him. I know that this kind of thinking steps over the line. Nevertheless, the need is still there, it's still real!

DOCTOR: This is not realistic thinking.

L.W.: Well, obviously not!

DOCTOR: Okay.

L.W.: Look Doc. I've always admitted that, "Well, okay, I'm screwed up for thinking this way,"and I've always been upfront with you about my state of mind. But I can't stop that I am thinking such thoughts, however bizarre they may be, even though they are not right nor realistic. You can't just say, "Oh, grow up, such thoughts are childish. " You wouldn't be a psychiatrist if you offered such simplistic answers.

DOCTOR: You're right. But one of the things we're doing here now is bringing more into your present thinking and making you more aware of the kind of thoughts you are having.

L.W.: Again, again and again and again, this need to be around and there for him. I know that he can't come to me. Harry Houdini proved that we can't return from beyond. Perhaps I'm thinking that if Allah can't come back to the mountain, the mountain may be able to go to him. Suicide was just a vehicle to get me there. You know, Doc; the more I talk, the sicker this all sounds! But I seem to be driven by passion, and reality has little to do with it.

DOCTOR: But this is being dramatic, it's being poetic, it's being—

L.W.: But I'm not doing this for effect, I'm not saying this to impress you.

DOCTOR: No, no, no. I understand that. But you are only directing this against yourself as a form of anger against yourself.

L.W.: Like self-flagelation.

DOCTOR: Masochism, if you want to call it that.

L.W.: It's also deep despair, that I really, really, and fundamentally, miss him!

DOCTOR: This has to do with part of your obsessive personality.

L.W.: Oh yeah. I take things to the "enth" degree!

DOCTOR: But you're hanging on to the death of your dad. We all have some hidden guilt about the death of our loved ones, because we are not perceptive. I can tell you stories about my own family.

L.W.: If I really want to be honest, Doc, I'm almost afraid of getting over all of this. It's like I want to freeze-frame, stop it all right here. I've never regarded myself as masochistic, and I know that's what all this sounds like. But getting over this hurdle would signal the start up of my life again, moving on, leaving him and perhaps the memory of it all behind. Reliving and re-telling the tragedy every week at my lectures keeps me immersed in the misery but it also keeps the memory alive. The bottom line, Doc, is I know he is dead, I just won't bury him. Yet, Doc, people keep telling me, after every lecture I do, just how well I've done with all of this, how well I've handled things; how much inner strength I display. They should only know that I never really dealt with this at all! I'm an imposter, I'm a fraud.

DOCTOR: Larry, let me interrupt you so that I can comment about a few things here. In the beginning of our session, you made comments relative to your job as well as this project that you're involved with, your book. You said that you felt that being a policeman wasn't good enough anymore, and that if you didn't get this book published you would be letting down your dad or at least his memory. You also talked at great length about this guilt you have about not being able to have prevented your dad's death.

Larry, first of all, consider all the things you have accomplished that other people merely dream about. First of all, you've surmounted a very traumatic childhood accident and though you were taunted and shut out, you also fought back and made people take notice of you. Some people quit after a bad relation-ship or marriage, but you persevered through three divorces and now look how far you've come, and how truly happy you are with Bonnie. You had a dream

140

about going to Tahiti, and you wound up fulfilling that dream, while others succeed in *only* dreaming! You've succeeded in earning a black belt in self-defense, certification in scuba diving, and now you are a certified pilot! Larry, most of us just dream about the adventures you've had and the achievements you've earned. So, you've accomplished a lot and you shouldn't be so down on yourself. As far as the book goes, the important thing to realize here is the fact that you tried. You know, there is something that's been said by greater philosophers than I, Larry. "If you're doing something, do it the best you can, no matter what it is." If you're making a mousetrap, you know, make a good one. If you're going to write a book, write the best one you can. If it's not accepted, it's not your fault, you did the best you can and this is what you have to tell yourself. With your dad, you did the best you could by offering your car. You did the best you could when you were protecting the town you were supposed to protect. You didn't have jurisdiction over the other town; you couldn't be in two places at the same time.

L.W.: I tell myself that, and I believe that. Yet it lies dormant, that latent guilt, which—

DOCTOR: All right, so now you know what's causing it, and you can tell yourself you are not guilty because you had no way on God's earth to get into two places at the same time. You couldn't persuade your dad to take the better car; you couldn't predict what would happen.

L.W.: But, forgetting all this, just the grief of missing somebody you love very much—which I've never really addressed myself to—when do you get over that? It's been over three years already. How do you get over the feeling of, well, gee, it was so good before, that, that . . . let me phrase this another way. When we we were all at Lake George was when I saw my father at his happiest. It was when we were the closest, the most fulfilled. He *was* the boat. He *was* the picnic on the island. He *was* the water-skiing, the scuba div-

141

ing. He *was* the enjoyment, all the good memories. Could it ever be just as good? In a different way? Any way? Do you know what I'm trying to ask? What I'm trying to say? I feel that if I had it the best, a good life, a good wife, *and* a father, then anything else is *less* than the best. This is why I feel, as I said at the beginning, that I have seen better days.

DOCTOR: Okay, when you go to Lake George, let me ask you this, Larry—do you have happy memories or are they—

L.W.: Happy memories.

DOCTOR: Do these happy memories then make you feel sad?

L.W.: Yes, very very melancholy.

DOCTOR: Now, why do you think that happens, Larry?

L.W.: Because he's not there anymore, to share those memories. He gave me my past and all the things we did together and all the places we went together. Well, he is just not there anymore, nor will he ever be.

DOCTOR: Can you accept that as a factor in reality, that he is not going to be there?

L.W.: Absolutely!

DOCTOR: All right, so since accepting that, do you think that by becoming depressed, it will help you in any way to see him back again, to help you—

L.W.: No. Can you be depressed just for the sake of being depressed, knowing full well that he is not coming back? Maybe I'm just afraid of being happy without him. Maybe it's that repressed guilt you mentioned, as if I *shouldn't* enjoy things now because ...

DOCTOR: In my way of thinking, Larry, it sums up to one thing. The reality testing of the situation is that your Dad is no longer with you. You had a good life with him while he was alive; the memories of Lake George are there to substantiate that. These are the memories that you want to have, and you must stop thinking beyond that state. There is nothing that you can control, beyond that state. This is the reality; you had this good life, they were happy memories. But to get depressed because he isn't there, this is a thing that should have been transient and resolved some time ago.

L.W.: Maybe I was thinking that there could never be any other kind of happiness without him. Because . . .

DOCTOR: What do people do to try to overcome this very feeling? What did they do about the Challenger that went up and killed all those people?

L.W.: They're going on, they'll put up another one.

DOCTOR: Fine. What else did they *do*?

L.W.: They gave them a memorial?

DOCTOR: Right! They made memorials for them, something to remember their memory, right?

L.W.: Right.

DOCTOR: Yes, they're all going to have feelings of sadness and eventually, it wears away, but the memorial remains. The memorial should be as pleasant of a memory as possible, of those times that you had that were both memorable and happy for you.

L.W.: I agree with what you're saying, Doc, but my memorial of my dad is the Lake George house that *he* designed and the boat that *he* worked hard for and enjoyed so much. They are, as you put it, memorials with pleasant memories. So pleasant and so affiliated with him that the memorials have now become shrines—things I regard as almost sacred! We want to sell the house because I'm building a new one. One that will have new, hopefully happy, memories. But I have such ambiguous feelings about that house, that I'm having—we're *all* having—problems reconciling with the sale. I know that it's just a thing, a "commodity to be bought and sold," as my father put it, but it's driving me nuts!

DOCTOR: Larry; what would your father say about—

L.W.: Doc, I know what you're going to ask. He would say, "Sell the damn house; the people in the house is all that matters." He would say, "Go on with your life."

DOCTOR: Which is very important, Larry. And how do you think he would feel if he knew you were thinking suicide?

L.W.: Oh, he'd kick me in the ass . . . figuratively, of course!

DOCTOR: Of course!

L.W.: Because he didn't go out and kill himself when his mother was killed, and no son loved a mother more! But despite his grief, Doc, he went on with his life. He raised a family and accomplished some extraordinary things. He helped a lot of people along the way. He never let life intimidate him. He would never just quit, Doc; he was no wimp!

DOCTOR: Well, Larry, I believe you just answered your own questions. How to go on with your life and how to pay your tribute to your father. Wouldn't you honor your father's memory more by doing exactly what he did in his time of despair? He went on, Larry. He went on and continued to live an active, full, and rewarding life. This is what he'd want you to do. Isn't this the appropriate tribute you've been looking for?

L.W.: Doc, like always, it's hard to argue with logic; your point has been made. So, let's assume that now I know better and, okay, you've saved a life. Now, how do I put the quality back into that life, how do I get back the enthusiasm? How does one ever find things as good as they once were after something like this? Or . . . well, let me rephrase that. Look, Doc, you had a father. You loved your father. There was something that you had, that you can never have again. There was something that you shared, that you will never share again. What did you do to replenish that fulfillment? What did you do to fill the void?

DOCTOR: Well, are you telling me, Larry, that you are looking for another father figure, that you're not as mature as you should be? You know, a father figure is somebody, as you grow up, you want to step on.

L.W.: No, Doc; I hope that's not what I'm saying, though it does pose an interesting possibility. Maybe I'm simply looking for someone to lean on right about now. You know, it's really odd that you would ask such a question.

DOCTOR: Why is that? Does the question make you feel uncomfortable?

L.W.: Yes, I suppose it does; it's a very compelling question. But it also reminded me of a very recent event. You know my friend Arthur?

DOCTOR: Of course.

L.W.: Well, he really doesn't act like any friend I've known; he's more like family. Anyway, I was having this problem. What that problem was really doesn't matter, and being the kind of guy he is, he wouldn't want anyone to know that he helped at all. Nonetheless, he picked up on my difficulty without me saying a word. He's intuitive that way, just like my father was; he's able to sense things. Then, like my father, he insisted that I allow him to help me. Then again, like my father, he didn't want to hear any thank-you's. He's a very selfless person, Doc, one of the good guys! Anyway, that night I called him up, but not to thank him for what he had done, but for what he had been to me that day.

DOCTOR: What had he been to you—a father figure?

L.W.: More than that, Doc, much more than that. His gesture didn't remind me of a father figure—he reminded me of my father! You know, for three years I had taken care of business—and in yeoman fashion I might add. I've been there for everybody else and have been tough for everyone else. Then, suddenly, I was able to lean on someone else. I had forgotten how good it felt to have someone else take charge. It was a luxury I hadn't enjoyed since my dad was killed. Maybe it's not that I miss the father figure so much. Maybe it's that I miss being able to be a "son"!

DOCTOR: Well, Larry, as you said before, you never stop being

145

a child until one of your parents is no longer around. Understand this too; growing up is an emotional thing, not a chronological thing. Just because we grow older it doesn't mean that we grow up. Because your father died suddenly, killed in such a gruesome manner, you had no time to prepare for this event. Being propelled from a sometimes dependent son to a full-time depended-upon adult is a traumatic experience at any age. Bear in mind, Larry, that so long as you remain a policeman, over 20,000 people regard you as their protector, often their father figure. You play this role at work, and now you're forced yourself to play this role model at home. You—

L.W.: Just a minute, Doc. Didn't you say before, that a father figure is somebody, as we are growing up, we want to step on?

DOCTOR: This is true.

L.W.: That's funny, Doc. I always wanted to know why people resent us so much. They call us quick enough when they are scared or bleeding. Then the very next day, if you give them a lousy $3.00 ticket, they go bananas—call you everything in the book!

DOCTOR: Well, Larry, you're the authority figure; you're the one who tells people, no, just like their parents told them. People, by nature, resent authority and police epitomize that authority.

L.W.: Okay, Doc. The next time I'm on duty and someone says, "Screw you," I'll smile at him and say, "Boy, I guess I remind him of his father!"

DOCTOR: Just understand that it's not you they resent, it's what you stand for. Now, getting back to this experience with Arthur. Having him take over, or take charge, gave you perhaps for the first time, an opportunity to vent. Venting is the essential part of your recovery. You see, Larry, what you have said so far has enhanced what psychiatrists call the "transference situation," which is part of the therapeutic process. In the transference, simply explained, you come to me and you see me as a father figure, someone that I resemble, or who compares to—

L.W.: Someone who has more wisdom than me, someone I respect.

DOCTOR: Whatever. Then the next approach has to be added to by the psychiatrist's feelings, where he begins to develop what is called the "countertransference." This is where he begins to see you as a son, or as a friend or as somebody he can get along with well, or he can relate to well, so you can develop a better relationship in the process. Do you follow me there? Because if we don't have that transference situation, it won't work as well, and this is what is going on between you and me. We've had this good relationship, and as a result, this is one of the reasons why, whatever these sessions have done for you, it has helped, I think. Each time I see you, you've come back stronger.

L.W.: Oh, yes, when I leave, I'm always more in focus of what's going on and just talking about it is therapy in itself. Up to this day, I never even admitted, even to myself, that I have a problem. This time, I even convinced myself that everything was cool. Look Doc, outwardly, I appear stoical, always in control. You know I'm a great pretender, the master of deception. I never like to telegraph weakness, and so, I never talked about it. I certainly wasn't about to say: "Hey, Mom" or "Guess what, Bonnie, I feel like putting a bullet in my head!" Knowing full well how much hurt I'd be putting on them, I elected to keep it all inside. So saying this all to you is saying it all for the first time. Now, if I could detach myself from myself, long enough to sit in your chair, I'd be thinking, "Boy, is this guy screwed up!" I don't like this situation at all. Whether it stems from the guilt or it's just out of exasperation, I'm fed up with this type of existence. Doc, I'm so close, or rather, I'm so receptive to hearing you say something, that will just snap me out of it.

DOCTOR: Larry, let me define this therapeutic process a little further, so you won't have to anticipate what you're expecting. The psychiatrist's role in the transference/

countertransference situation, is a passive one. This whole business is called the "talking treatment." The patient talks, he hears himself talk, and he solves his problems. The psychiatrist guides you, getting some of the problems out of the unconscious, so you can help solve those problems.

L.W.: I understand exactly what you're saying and yes, in years past, this procedure has worked well and the quality of my life has always improved. It's just this one time that I seem to be stalled. Doc, your Dad died an unfortunate death. Do you ever really get over it?

DOCTOR: No, Larry, you never get over the loss of a loved one. However, the mature person is able to go on, and that's what your father would have wanted you to do. Killing yourself or tormenting yourself as you are doing is pathological behavior. Once again, the proper tribute to your father would be to live out a full and happier life. Make the tribute of your book count. You'll accomplish this by having your message *save* lives, but certainly not by taking your own! All that would do is hurt those who have hurt too much already, the ones you love the most. This would be a cruel thing to do to those people and I've never known you to be cruel. Look, Larry, it's unfortunate that death occurs, but it's something that is a part of life. You can't have life without death. You can't have . . . there I go again, philosophizing.

L.W.: No, Doc, I like that. Go on.

DOCTOR: You can't have day without having night. Some day I'll write my theory that "life" is a bifacial existence. You have good, you have bad, you have happiness, you have sadness. Everything has an opposite.

L.W.: The Yin and Yang, two opposites that coexist harmoniously.

DOCTOR: Of course, and if you don't have death you wouldn't be, because there would be no such thing as life.

L.W.: Kind of reminds me of taking that horrible boat ride from Tahiti. I had waited so long to go, a dream come true. But to have journeyed so far only to succumb to that awful, seasick feeling. But in my moment of desperation, this fellow passenger remarked, you can't enjoy the ups in life unless you've experienced the downs!

DOCTOR: Exactly.

L.W.: But by the same token, if I didn't have it so good before, I wouldn't be so miserable now. Because that's what's hurting me right now—all those good memories.

DOCTOR: But what you're doing here now is turning those good memories into bad things because you are using them masochistically, to hurt yourself, rather than to think of those memories as a pleasant experience, which they were in reality.

L.W.: But the memories are a two-edged sword.

DOCTOR: Yes, but you're cutting yourself with that two-edged sword. You're directing the worst part at you. Why can't you use those pleasant memories to enjoy the thought of your dad instead of feeling bad about all of this? It's not easy. I can talk to you about it, but I can't have you do it unless you can overcome it yourself.

L.W.: Do you yourself feel that way, with the memory of your father? Are you still bitter?

DOCTOR: I'm angry as to what went on at that hospital. I'm sorry that I had no control over it.

L.W.: That's what I hate—having no control over the situation. You feel violated.

DOCTOR: That's it, but I wasn't told anything, I was kept in the dark about it. This is what happens when you depend on other people. Like when you depended on this driver who killed your father. You depended on him not to be drinking at the time. He was supposed to be responsible but he was out of control. The controlled situation would have been for this man not to be driving under the influence and if it were the case, this tragedy wouldn't have happened.

L.W.:   But because he couldn't control his life, we had to suffer and now it controls my life. But in the future, Doc, I *will* try to savor all the good memories and I'll try and honor my dad in more constructive ways. I promise that I'll try.

These sessions were conducted on February 4, 1986 in the office of Dr. Feldman, in Livingston, New Jersey. As well as being a police psychiatrist, Dr. Feldman is Clinical Associate Professor at New Jersey College of Medicine & Dentistry.

POSTSCRIPT

It's been said that 90 percent of resolving a problem is admitting that one exists. The doctor got me to admit certain truths, and many of those things that were plaguing me have been resolved. Sometimes however, the cure for a problem can be remedied by the problem itself. Take for instance a poisonous snake bite. The antidote for the bite is manufactured from the venom of yet another poisonous snake. Even after the sessions with the police psychiatrist, I was still watching excessive amounts of T.V., my buffer from reality. But something was telling me that if I didn't get out of that seat in front of the tube soon, it would have to be surgically removed from my butt! Then came something of a revelation...A show I was watching had inspired me to start living without this visual aid.

After my father's death, I became a fan of all works produced by Michael Landon. Like "Star Trek," the show "Little House on the Prairie" removed me from the present and propelled me into another time frame. This time it was back instead of ahead. As long as it wasn't "now," it didn't seem to matter. Maybe I liked "Walnut Grove" because there were no cars, nothing to remind me of our family's triple tragedy. The show was very soothing, and if it didn't have a happy ending, at least it had a moral one. I, being a hopeless idealist, just loved seeing "right" prevail for a change. But the show also had a therapeutic value. It got me to demonstrate and vent feelings that I wouldn't allow myself to show or feel on my own. How odd it was that I could appear so stoical over the loss of my father, yet I cried when Albert, the fictionalized son in the show, died of leukemia. As soon as the episode was over, the facade would once again go up and I would continue to deny my own personal hurts.

The inspiration to go on with my life came from yet another Landon production. It was his autobiographical piece called "Sam's Son." As a child, Landon was also ridiculed, as I had been.

151

Young Michael was well acquainted with the loneliness and torments that were the byproducts of peer pressure. He too sought escape through the exploits of his movie heroes. Like me, he loved and revered his father second to none. The movie was a tribute to a father by his loving son. As a direct result of his work, I was inspired to make a lasting tribute to my father and that's exactly how this book got started. Instead of just admiring this man's creation, I decided to admire the man who created it! The T.V. went off and I picked up the pen. Thank you, Mr. Landon.

From time to time I read or see other people who are trying to make a difference—Mrs. Reagan, people in Hollywood such as Stevie Wonder, Brooke Shields, Mariette Hartley. There are more, but these are just a few who could have just as easily sat back and done absolutely nothing; they certainly didn't need the fame or the money. If everybody had their conscience or shared their concerns for their fellow human beings, people like my father might still be alive today. My heartfelt thanks extends to these people as well.

Starting a project is one thing; completing it is something entirely different. As one who has quit a lot more things than he started, this too represents a triumph as well as a tribute. You have seen what inspired me to start this project; now I want to thank the person who unwittingly kept it going. When I had completed just one sample chapter, I sought to elicit responses from a cross-section readership. I wanted the style of writing to appeal to just about anyone who possessed a driver's license. Their comments often dictated the direction of the story line. One of those who provided me with a candid response was our own township magistrate, the Honorable James Haggerty. But before I tell you what the judge said, let me refer back to a Phil Donahue episode mentioned earlier in this story. It dealt with coping with the loss of a loved one. The comment that intrigued me the most touched upon the need to seek a parent's approval, even from beyond the grave. Throughout this project, people constantly reminded me how proud my father would have been. They said he "would have been" pleased to see that because of his death and my book, others might be spared a like tragedy. Their comments reflected Dad's caring personality; they gave me the posthumous "pat on the head," the "approval" I had been looking for. This book represents a personal tribute to my dad but, selfishly, I wanted to accomplish something that would have made my father proud of me. Yet this has been the book that almost wasn't.

Despite the initial comments and compliments, I suddenly realized that all those "would have beens" wasn't going to cut it. After all, the *only* person I sought praise from was no longer around. Suddenly, there was no more incentive, no more reward, so I stopped writing. But then came a very strange encounter with Judge Haggerty. In his private chambers he handed me back my original outline and sample chapter. In his usual calm and deliberate manner, he started to give me his critique of my project. I had anticipated the polite but usual "your father would have been proud" speech. In this case however, the judge rendered a different verdict. He said, "You know Larry, your father is very proud of you right now." I was extremely taken aback by his use of the word "is," as if he were speaking in the present tense. But he said it so casually and so matter-of-factly, that I had to believe that he actually meant it! In the past, I had not always agreed with the judge's decisions, but this was one conclusion I was happy to sustain. From that day on, I have felt that my father has been watching. I had my required audience and renewed determination to complete what I had started. Thanks, Judge, and thanks, Bonnie for cheering me on throughout this entire effort. Couldn't have done it without you!

My original intentions were to *include* you in this story. I didn't want you to merely read about it, I wanted you to *feel* it and experience what it's actually like to be victimized by the drunk driver. You now have come as close as one can to this story without actually bleeding. All the points I wanted to make have already been made. I hope you have realized that I'm not a prohibitionist. I'm not against drinking. I am staunchly opposed to drinking and driving drunk, and to the consumption of any drug for purposes of escape from one's problems or oneself. Let's not forget the real villain of this story—peer pressure, the number one reason for taking that initial drink (or whatever) in the first place. How many of you are willing to ruin your lives or have done so already, just to please others? This is why I'm against the consumption of liquor by our nation's youth—it always begins for all the wrong reasons.

In that neverending quest for escape today, we risk cheating others of any tomorrow, and at the very least, waste our precious time. I offered myself as the best example of wasted time. You observed how I used dreams and illusions to hide from problems. But I've also demonstrated tht ultimate fulfillment can *only* be achieved through *reality*. It's okay to have dreams in life, providing that those dreams don't run your life. I opted to exchange unobtainable dreams for very achievable goals. Throughout this story, I've tried to appeal to your common sense. If that hasn't worked, then in light of how this tragedy has devastated the lives of innocent people, perhaps I can appeal to your conscience. If after all this effort you still aren't moved, my story may indeed become *your* story.

My brother's close friend, Douglas M. Fondo, a Connecticut resident, was struck head on by a drunk driver on November 6, 1985 and was killed. Doug was an athlete, a scholar, a leader. But above all, he was a good person. He was also the son of Mr. and Mrs. Michael Fondo. It is said that when one loses a parent, that person loses their past. But when a child is lost, a parent loses their future. It took me just a few months to write about a past that once was. The Fondos will have to endure a lifetime of what might have been, and that has to be worse.

I beg you, stop the suffering and senseless killings:

DON'T DRIVE DRUNK

———————————— □ ————————————

SPECIAL OFFER

to any group that is concerned with the problem
of drunk driving, and the associated problems of
alcoholism and other drug abuse.
The publisher will offer a special discount
to help in fundraising ventures or other drives
that help to spread the message
DON'T DRIVE DRUNK
* * *

for information contact:
Waimon Publishing
7 Quinby Court
Parsippany, NJ 07054
Tel: (201) 428-9352